3 9153 00940192 0

W9-BNB-349

THE REVOLUTIONARY THEME IN
CONTEMPORARY AMERICA

A CENTENNIAL PUBLICATION

THE REVOLUTIONARY THEME IN CONTEMPORARY AMERICA

BY *MAX LERNER, SEYMOUR MARTIN LIPSET, C. HERMAN PRITCHETT, & PETER F. DRUCKER*
EDITED BY THOMAS R. FORD

1965 · LEXINGTON, KENTUCKY
UNIVERSITY OF KENTUCKY PRESS

Copyright © 1965 by the University of Kentucky Press
Manufactured in the United States of America
Library of Congress Catalog Card Number
65-27013

INTRODUCTION

THE FOUR PAPERS included in this volume were originally presented at a conference held at the University of Kentucky in April of 1965 as one of the events marking the celebration of the University's Centennial. The purpose of the conference was established in the official message of the University's President, John W. Oswald, inaugurating the observation of the Centennial when he observed: "Our Centennial Year is an important occasion in that it is a time for reflection with pride on past achievements. More importantly, however, it is a time to ascertain the role we must play in the affairs of the community, state, and nation during the next one hundred years."

The role of a university, especially that of a state university, cannot be comprehended apart from the society which it serves; and the formidable but necessary task of charting the future of a university requires more than a superficial consideration of what is taking place (or should take place) in the total society to which it has so much to contribute. To help stimulate thought about the nature and implications of the complex social changes which today are occurring with such rapidity, four distinguished scholars whose previous work had demonstrated their deep concern for America's future society were invited to participate in a two-day public conference devoted to the theme "Main Currents in American Life." It is significant that the connecting bond of the papers

contributed by these four scholars—Max Lerner, Seymour Martin Lipset, C. Herman Pritchett, and Peter
Drucker—was a common interest in what might be called
the revolutionary spirit in contemporary America.

This theme, of course, has been recurrent throughout
our national history. From Jefferson onward, thoughtful
men have pondered whether the spirit of excitement,
idealism, promise and hope in which the Great Experi-
ment of Democracy was launched could long endure. The
doubts of—and fears for—its continued existence were
probably never more clearly expressed than by Alexis de
Tocqueville in *Democracy in America:*

If men continue to shut themselves more closely within
the narrow circle of domestic interests and to live upon that
kind of excitement, it is to be apprehended that they may
ultimately become inaccessible to those great and powerful
emotions which perturb nations, but which enlarge and recruit
them. When property becomes so fluctuating, and the love of
property so restless and so ardent, I cannot but fear that men
may arrive at such a state as to regard every new theory as a
peril, every innovation as an irksome toil, every social im-
provement as a stepping-stone to revolution, and so refuse to
move altogether for fear of having moved too far. I dread,
and I confess it, lest they should at last so entirely give way to
a cowardly love of present enjoyment, as to lose sight of the
interests of their future selves and of those of their de-
scendants; and to prefer to glide along the easy current of
life, rather than to make, when it is necessary, a strong and
sudden effort to higher purpose.

Complacency—that insidious arch-enemy of social progress—is perhaps in our current age of affluence a greater
threat than ever before. But the fact remains, as Max
Lerner points out in his opening essay, that we are still
living in a revolutionary time. And like the revolutions
of the 18th century, the present one is multi-faceted: social,

economic, technological, political, cultural. Mr. Lerner elaborates upon six aspects of social change which he calls the *revolution of weapons technology,* the *revolution of access,* the *uprooting revolution,* the *cultural and intellectual explosions,* the *time revolution,* and the *revolution of values.* Each of these revolutions simultaneously holds promises and poses threats not only for American civilization but for the entire world. "Our problem," Mr. Lerner states, "is to locate these revolutionary changes, to channel them, to tame them to the uses of a radical humanism. . . ."

Whether or not our society will effectively deal with this problem, Mr. Lerner does not say. In his own words, he is neither an optimist nor a pessimist, but a "possibilist." The kind of resolution which we eventually achieve, if we do achieve one, will undoubtedly depend in large measure on the outcome of the *values revolution.* The background of this revolution is carefully analyzed by Seymour Martin Lipset in his comparison of value themes in the United States and Canada. "Many writers seeking to account for value differences between the United States and Canada," Mr. Lipset observes, "suggest they stem in large part from the revolutionary origin of the United States and the counter-revolutionary history of Canada, from two disparate founding ethos."

Although value differences stemming from the disparate ideologies which emerged during the American Revolution still persist, Mr. Lipset is candid in reporting that the revolutionary image of the United States has faded drastically: "Relatively few in the rest of the world still see the United States in the idealistic terms with which it views itself. To the leaders of the underdeveloped and the Communist world, the United States is now the leading defender of conservative traditional social forms, and is governed from within by an oligarchy or power-elite."

The extent to which the changed image of the United States in the eyes of the world actually represents an underlying reality is a matter of crucial concern. Are we merely the victims of distortion? Or have we brought to realization the fears expressed by Tocqueville that "modern society . . . will ultimately be too invariably fixed in the same institutions," its people unwilling to make that "strong and sudden effort to higher purpose?" At least to one recent foreign observer, Father Bruckberger—a compatriot of Tocqueville some three generations removed—there is some truth in both interpretations. In his *Image of America,* Father Bruckberger concedes that Communist propaganda has drawn a "horrible caricature" of America. But he also warns of the imminent peril to the entire West stemming from our failure to carry through quickly the unfinished business of American democracy because of "those delays, those cautious measures, those formulas for compromise at which your politicians so excel." And no business, in Father Bruckberger's view, requires more immediate attention than that of granting Negro citizens "their right to frank and fraternal acceptance in the community."

Perhaps there is no stronger evidence of the persistence of the revolutionary spirit than the tremendous progress made in the claiming and implementation of the rights of the Negro minority in the short period of some six years since Father Bruckberger published his warning and appeal. What is most surprising of all, though—and in many ways most heartening—is that the critical impetus toward the achievement of these rights came from the Supreme Court, that venerable organ of American government which a scant generation ago was a classic example, at least from the viewpoint of American liberals, of an institution "too invariably fixed."

The amazing transition of the Supreme Court from

the "brake" to the "motor" of public policy and its implications are thoughtfully traced by C. Herman Pritchett
in his essay on "The Judicial Revolution and American
Democracy." In the course of his analysis, he also provides substantial confirmation of Max Lerner's *revolution
of access*. The accessibility of the judicial process to
individuals and minorities, Mr. Pritchett points out, is
perhaps more important for democratic theory than any
other feature.

The *revolution of access* is not restricted to the judicial
process, however. The impact of its tremendous and
increasing force is also being experienced by our institutions of higher education, as Peter Drucker reports in
his essay "The Revolution in Higher Education." "Today," he observes, "half of the young men in America
go to school beyond high school. . . . Tomorrow we can
expect a college degree to have become as common for
both sexes as the high school degree was only two decades
ago."

The demands of the "Educated Society" of tomorrow
hold implications for the university that are themselves
revolutionary, and Mr. Drucker specifies some of the
drastic changes he feels must take place. Most challenging
of all is his view that the university must become more
than our primary institution for the production and
transmission of higher knowledge; it must serve as the
very center of our society.

Viewed collectively, there can be little doubt that the
four papers presented herein serve well their original
intent of stimulating thought about the future course of
our society and the role the university is to play in it. If
they offer no clear auguries of the future, which in truth
they do not, it is partly because of their implicit rejection
(explicitly stated by Max Lerner) of simplistic determinism. The course of the future, as always, is one of possi-

bilities; and for our society to prevail, we must continuously re-assess those possibilities, remaining ever-willing to make the "strong and sudden effort to higher purpose." If Peter Drucker is correct in his judgment, the responsibility for making the assessments and for guiding the decisions will be increasingly delegated to the university as the vital institution of our future society. And, as Max Lerner so cogently reminds us, the role of the university must not be that of simply mirroring the changes of our civilization, but of mastering them and subjecting them to humanistic ends.

Because the issues raised here are of such moment not only to other universities but to our society, our civilization, the University of Kentucky takes this means of giving them wider circulation. In so doing, it re-affirms the belief of the philosophic father of the spirit of the American revolution, Thomas Jefferson, that "the information of the people at large can alone make them the safe, as they are the sole, repository of our freedom."

THOMAS R. FORD

CONTENTS

SIX REVOLUTIONS IN
AMERICAN LIFE

BY MAX LERNER

WE MEET IN A PERIOD of the breaking and making of nations and the testing of civilizations. The historian will have to call our era a time of the shaking of the foundations. When we speak of ours as a revolutionary time, there are two meanings of the term revolution which we are in danger of confusing. One refers to a transfer of power, perhaps from one class to another, as a result of a direct action. In the second sense, revolution means a drastic, highly accelerated pace of change— so rapid as to effect a breakthrough, then to create a new level from which further cumulative changes take place.

It is curious that so many Americans in our own time should recoil both from the term and the idea of revolution. Clearly the authentic revolution of modern history, even in the first sense, has been the American Revolution, which was not a revolution with a stick, but a revolution with consent. Even more clearly America is a revolutionary civilization in the second sense. It took me a little over a decade to write *America as a Civilization,* and I found when I came to the end of that decade that a number of things I had written at the beginning about America were no longer valid. The American civilization had been changing drastically right under my fingertips as I was writing about it—and as it continues to do today. Our problem is to locate these revolutionary changes, to channel them, to tame them to the uses of radical humanism, using the term *radical* in the sense that man

1

is the root of all changes and the measure of all utilities. It is within the frame of such revolutions both in America and in the world outside, that we shall have to carry out not only the planned and channeled social changes I have spoken of, but also whatever little insurrections of the mind and spirit we can manage within ourselves, inside of our own psyches.

I am happy to have been asked to come here, and to help you celebrate your centennial, because a university is a convergence point of the major revolutionary forces of our time. It is true that the university is a subculture within itself. But it is a special kind of subculture—the kind which must not simply mirror the changes in the civilization, but must master them and subject them to the uses of human beings.

The American civilization into which we are now moving—computer-geared, information-directed, leisure-oriented—will, I trust, be an authentic revolutionary society. But we must make certain that it will not be simply a brave new world squeezed dry of human values, a world in which automation results in a kind of automated man. I have a dream, and I dare to dream it on a university campus. It is a dream of possibility, of a possible emergent man in the American civilization: one who will be a revolutionary in the sense that he will meet the changes of his time with an unsurprised alertness; one who will not recoil from the machine, from technology, from power, from changes, from the reality principle in a world which is neither a graceful nor a gracious world; one who, along with that realism, will not allow himself to become dehumanized; one who will put out antennae of sensibility to pick up the new tremors that make themselves felt in the life of the mind and spirit; one who will not succumb to the fanaticism of the True Believer in an age of ideology, and yet also one who will know the values that

2

he is committed to; one who will be a unique individual in a society of diversity, but one who will also know that man can become a monster unless he forges the humane nexus that ties him with his fellow-man.

II

Having shared this not-impossible dream with you, let me sketch out what I have been rash enough to designate as six major revolutions of our time. I deal first with the *revolution of weapons technology,* as part of the larger technological revolution of our time. I called a recent book of mine *The Age of Overkill,* because the weapons now at the command of the Great Powers carry with them the overkill factor, the capacity to over-destroy their target many times. The Russians and ourselves today have weapons enough to over-destroy not only each other, but humanity itself. Machiavelli gave us a grammar of power tracing out for successive centuries the system of classical politics in an age of nation-states. And just as in classical economics the crucial concept was the scarcity of wealth, so in the system of classical politics the crucial concept was that of the scarcity of power. Each nation, each head of state, could never get power enough, but had to pile power on power until finally war came with its test and showdown of power.

That is no longer possible. What these overkill weapons have done has been to transform a realm of power scarcity into a realm of power surplus. It is true, at any rate of the major nuclear powers, that they now have more power at their command than they can use or dare use. This does not mean, because the use of these weapons is unthinkable, that it is therefore impossible. History has shown us on a number of occasions that the unthinkable sometimes happens, that the unthinkable does take

3

place. But in terms of calculated decisions, these weapons have become unusable. Power, paradoxically, has become powerless. The wars in the calculable future, like the war in Vietnam, are likely to be wars not with nuclear but with conventional weapons, although there is the shadowy possibility of the use of nuclear weapons. In this era in which power has become powerless, we need to rethink the meaning of the nation-state and of absolute national sovereignty.

I recall a conversation with Wendell Willkie, shortly after Hiroshima. From now on, he said, national sovereignty is no longer something to be hoarded, but something to be spent. This is true of everything important in life—of love and affection between parents and children, between husband and wife, between intimate friends. If you try to hoard it, and dole it out with a kind of *quid pro quo,* you find yourself ending up loveless and unloved. But if you spend it generously, you find that you end with more than you started. If we try to hoard sovereignty, if we say "Get the United States out of the United Nations and the United Nations out of the United States," if we ask what concern it is of ours that there are have-not nations in the world, if we ask why we should take the trouble to shape the links that will tie us within an organic community someday with our allies in Western Europe or our neighbors to the South of us; if we ask these things, then we will find ourselves hugging our absolute sovereignty to our breast while we sit on top of a mound of radiated ashes. But if we surrender enough of our sovereign power to a common decision-making pool, say with our allies in Western Europe and ultimately with others, we can develop a scrambled or pooled sovereignty to serve as a frame within which we can nail down the future.

Along with the erosion of absolute sovereignty there

4

has been a considerable erosion of ideology. In a large part of the Communist world, especially in the Soviet Union and Eastern Europe, a new skepticism has developed, but alongside it there is also a new ideological fanaticism among the Chinese Communists and their tributaries. Within this frame of ideological erosion and renewal, a revolution of polycentricism has taken place within the Communist power-cluster, in the form of a split between the Russians and the Chinese in their struggle for the mastery of the Communist camp. This gives us, luckily, a chance to practice the arts not so much of military as of political warfare, not so much of the arms race as of the intelligence race. Given this split between the Russians and the Chinese, we may have a chance in the calculable future to develop something like a Concert of Powers, not an alliance but a meeting of minds between ourselves and the Great Powers of Western Europe, the Soviet Union, India, Japan, China itself—if China will come into such a concert. It would first be directed toward preventing the further diffusion of nuclear weapons, then toward arms control and disarmament, and finally toward a collective world authority, including a world policing force. Until we have done that we will not have managed to give ourselves tolerable assurance of lasting peace. If we can do that then we can finish some of the unfinished business of democracy in our own civilization.

As an American I care deeply about some of the cultural creativeness that we have already developed and even more about the potential that we still have. I spoke of a world policing force, not of a world state nor of a homogenized world society. I do not want to see a homogenized world society which would blot out the cultural differences between nations, any more than I want to see a homogenized American society that blots out the diversities of individuals and groups. I am a cultural nationalist in the sense that I care deeply about the contribution that American civilization can make to the world culture pool.

A great deal of the overkill shadow of our time hangs over our young people, obscuring their vision, making them wonder whether they have an operational claim to the future. When I am asked whether I am an optimist or a pessimist about the future, I answer that in our collective affairs it is not in our stars but in ourselves that we shape our future—within our collective intelligence and our collective will.

I am neither an optimist nor a pessimist, I am a possibilist. I believe that it will be possible to prevent nuclear catastrophe, possible to prevent totalitarian tyranny, possible to shape a shared, pooled sovereignty. But none of these is guaranteed. When I write and teach history, I see not only the decisions that were made in the past and the consequences that followed, but also the decisions that were not made, the roads not taken, and what might have happened if they had been. As I look toward the future, I see the future as possibility, depending upon the decisions that are made and upon our collective intelligence and will.

The future does not belong to capitalism nor to communism nor to socialism nor any of the other prescriptive varieties of society and state. The future belongs to various forms of welfarism, in the sense of the new imperative for the state and society to care about the welfare of the individual. We have the possibility of sharing the fruits of our technology inside our own society as equitably as possible, and with other societies as well. "In my father's house there are many mansions." There will be many mansions of welfarism, provided that none is aggressive, provided that they live up to the collective con-

6

science of mankind. We can claim the future if we see it in these terms.

III

There can be no sharing of welfare unless there is equal access to it. That is why I call the second revolution of our time, the *revolution of access*. In exploring space and getting new glimpses of the spacious firmament on high, we have had some of it rub off into a new ferment about a spacious society in America. President Johnson has mapped out some outlines of the "Great Society." They have to do with the attack on poverty and on the slums, with transportation, with urban rebuilding, with educational opportunity, especially in giving the children of the poor a new chance. They have to do with breakdown in the community, with addiction, with alcoholism, with various aspects of the ills of our society.

There are some who will say that there have always been poverty, inequality, slums, and always will be; that life is tragic, but that little can be done about it. My answer is: don't demean the word *tragic*. Tragedy is a grander, nobler concept. It is a part of the very constitution of the universe. No man, no nation is immune to tragedy. But there is a difference between the tragic and the pathetic. The tragic is part of the constitution of the universe, outside man's control; the pathetic is man-made, and because it is man-made it can be man-resolved. We will never eliminate the tragic from life. But we can make sure of whittling away the pathetic. Poverty is not tragic, it is pathetic. The slums are not tragic, they are pathetic. Alcoholism, drug addiction, the breakdown of the neighborhood: these are not tragic, they are pathetic. Racial hatred and discrimination, religious bigotry, war itself, are man-made, and can be man-resolved.

Men are not equal. I recall an evening I had some years

7

ago with a number of journalists and professors in Warsaw. The chairman said, "Mr. Lerner, we know of your book on American civilization. We haven't had a chance to have it translated. But could you tell us in one word what is the essence of American civilization?" I was startled. "This is a book of a thousand pages," I said, "You want me to distill it into one word?" He said, "That's right."

I thought very rapidly. Is it freedom? Equality? Democracy? Dynamism? Suddenly I heard myself say, "Access." The chairman laughed: "We have heard of American *success,* but not of American *access."* I said, "We have a Declaration of Independence which says that all men are born free and equal. I hope we are born free, and will remain free. But we are not born equal. We are born very unequal, with unequal abilities and potentials. Every employer knows it, every army commander, every teacher, every parent knows it. Every one of my own children was born with unequal abilities and potentials—not racial or religious or sectional difference, but individual differences. But we also have the notion that there ought to be equal access to opportunity, so that every one of these unequally born youngsters gets a chance to develop his unequal abilities to the full."

My parents came from Russia a long time ago. Why did they bring their little brood with them to America? Not to get rich, although there was a legend among immigrants that in America the paving stones themselves were made of gold. They came so that their children would get an equal chance at a chance. I have had it, and my children are having it. We cannot rest content until every young American gets that equal chance. The burden and the opportunity lie heavy on our conscience.

The civil rights revolution of our time is an effort to make these equal life chances accessible to all, so that they can face the tragedy of life as well as the creative-

8

ness of life. In that sense it is part of the revolution of access.

What I have been describing is not the Great Society. It is a welfare society, a necessary effort to build a floor below which the human condition is not allowed to fall. Beyond welfarism there is potentially a spacious society. But it has to do not so much with achieving a consensus for legislation, as with forging a bond among Americans.

IV

This leads to the third revolution—an *uprooting revolution* which makes it difficult to develop the whole person within a healthy culture. We have grown more aware of this recently, with the pervasive violence of our time, with the breaking of internal controls and internalized standards, with a certain normlessness that has set in. Americans have been uprooted from the soil, the farm, the small towns, the neighborhood, the city core, from religion, from their codes and traditions, from the cohesive family. This is part of the price they have had to pay for the freedoms of a society that cherishes free choices, and for drastically accelerated changes in that society.

There was a time when we thought that the ills of a society came from sin and the violation of God's moral law: this was a sort of determinism as a single-factor analysis of the source of change in society. More recently this was succeeded by an economic determinism, which later was broadened out into an environmental determinism. There are still sociologists who tell us that crime, delinquency, violence come out of poverty and the slums, and that if we were to eliminate poverty and the slums, we would eliminate these products of theirs. There is a core of truth here, but I feel that we need a subtler and

9

deeper approach which sees that the personality operates in the culture and the culture in the personality. The same cultural and environmental pressures upon different personalities produce different results, just as the same personality structure set in different cultural environments leads to different personal outcomes.

Given this approach, I turn to the nature of our uprooting revolution and some of the things that happen as a consequence to the personality. I select from the large mass of cultural pressures three in particular. I call them assaults on the identity of the individual.

One assault comes from the big media. While I am not one of those who make the big media responsible for every ill in our society, I am concerned about their consequences for the personality. In the case of television, what counts is not the quality, but the size of the audience that is sold to a sponsor. Every head counts for one, no matter what's inside of it. This is the principle of replaceable parts and therefore the principle of naked mechanism. Immanuel Kant asked to have human beings treated as subjects, not as objects. But the principle of replaceable parts treats them as objects, not as subjects. If the aim is to build a big audience, the appeal to the violent and destructive in each of us becomes part of the means. The result is too well known for me to underscore.

The second assault is the assault from big organizations. We find ourselves increasingly part of the over-organized in society which is replacing the organic. This is true of big universities, just as it is true of big government, big corporations, big trade unions, big churches, big law firms, big hospitals. We are going to have to live with big organizations and work in them. But to live with them and to work in them does not mean to live by their values nor to live by their pressures. We have a chance to insist that organization will not carry with it conformity, that bureaucracy will not carry with it routineering. We must dare to become anarchists of a new kind—to care deeply about the individual as against the abstraction, to cultivate the small organic group as a life-core, even while we live with the over-organized massive unit.

Finally there is the assault from the disintegrated, uprooted family. Every student of the American family knows that the traditional family was not only a consuming and a residential unit, but also a producing unit, a working unit, an educational unit. I have had occasion recently to write about the vanishing American father. He is a vanishing father in a double sense: first the quite physical sense that he is not there much, except after work and on week-ends, and sometimes not even then; second, that the emotional and intellectual authority of the father inside the family is waning. To some extent the mother has come in as a kind of surrogate, adding to the already burdened life of the American woman, perhaps the most burdened creature in the whole history of womankind. But often even the mother is ineffectual, and what has been left has been a vacuum of authority. With that vacuum of authority there comes a vacuum of identity and belief. Under these conditions it is hard to grow up in America, hard to shape adequately a sense of identity.

The pervasive violence of our time comes largely from two groups. One is the rebels with a cause who, because of their deep belief in their cause (one thinks of the civil rights revolution), are willing to challenge local ordinances and grapple with the police if necessary. There is also a second kind of violence, that of the "rebels without a cause" (the phrase is Dr. Robert Lindner's) who are largely responsible for the violence on the streets and

11

on subways in the big urban sprawl. These two forms of violence are not commensurate; it would be a great mistake to confuse them. Each presents a problem, but they are incommensurate problems. The deep problem of our time is that of the rebels without a cause.

This does not mean that the two problems are unrelated. In many cases—I think of Harlem and the Stuyvesant-Bedford area and the Watts ghetto—there is a smoldering sense of grievance, an identification with the grievance of the whole racial group against the society. I go back here to an insight from Tocqueville's *Ancien Régime and the French Revolution,* where he pointed out that the French Revolution came not when the condition of the peasantry was at its worst, but when it was improving. In that sense the French Revolution was a revolution of rising expectations, to use our modern term. This is also true of what is happening in America today. A good part of the violence that comes from the ethnically and economically depressed areas comes from people whose conditions are not deteriorating but are improving. Their living standards are rising; but because they are getting a glimpse of the possibilities of life in an American civilization with all of its Babylonian richness, its sensuousness, its luxury, they feel themselves shut out from so much that remains, and they try to wreak their frustrations upon the society as a whole. Thus some of the violence of our country comes from the residual gap which the ethnic minorities still feel—the gap between the actual and the potential.

Much of the violence, however, especially of the rebels without a cause, is part of the generational conflict. There are many people who feel that intelligent beings on other planets are trying to send some kind of a message, some communication from interplanetary space, and that we ought to lay ourselves open to this message. Right now

12

I am more concerned about another message coming to us, not from space but from our young people. They are trying to call our attention to this gap between the actual and the potential. They do not find in their own experience that American civilization is a credible civilization.

Eric Erickson has said that in the adolescent years there is a great craving for fidelity, the craving to find someone to trust, someone who will trust you. One of the young men in the riots on the University of California campus warned his listeners, "Don't trust anyone over thirty." It is a portent that fidelity between the generations has broken down, and that walls of non-communication have been built up.

Some parents and teachers and preachers and others tend to think that much of this violence is due to a kind of diabolism, that the Devil has entered into our young people and is working his will. I have never gone for any devil theory either of history or society, and I don't believe that it is an illuminating theory in the present instance. I believe that these young people do have something to say to us, that they want teaching teachers, parenting parents, effective models, older people they can trust in a society that has meaning. If we can once establish that these are possible for them, we can in turn ask them for their trust in ourselves and in our society and in the possibilities of their lives in that society.

What is happening today on a number of campuses seems to me to be not only meaningful but valuable in this sense. There are excesses doubtless in what is happening, but they seem marginal. The crucial fact is the effort on the part of our young people once more to make themselves a functioning part of what is happening around them. I can recall in the early 1930's a college generation that was socially conscious. Then there was a period when they became very self-conscious, very psyche-conscious.

13

And then there was a period when they became uncon-
scious. I am glad they have moved out of that stage, into
the socially conscious again.

The young people, with all their marching, may ultimately learn where they want to go. They may, out of
their sitting, develop some kind of contemplative life.
Mr. Justice Holmes once said, "It is required of a man
that he should share the passion and the action of his time,
at peril of being judged not to have lived." I think
what is happening to the young Americans on college
campuses is that they are trying to share in the passions
and actions of their time—lest they feel that they have not
lived.

V

This leads me to the *cultural and intellectual explosions*
that are taking place, and which gave a new revolutionary
frame to the functioning of the elites. Things are happening within our society which may bring within our
reach a chance to build a life with content and a sense
of selfhood. I am thinking of the knowledge explosion,
the education explosion, the paperback and reading revolution, the communications explosion, the cultural explosion. Things are happening also to the carriers of
what is creative in these explosions.

America is not only a mass culture. If it were only that,
then a good part of what is easy, sleazy and vendible,
nerveless and homogenized about our mass culture would
characterize the whole of the American culture. America
is an elite culture as well. In a sense we are becoming an
education society. As President Oswald said in his opening
remarks, the education revolution is today largely a
quantitative one; our task is to make it also a qualitative
one. What is confusing us is that the class education axis
has shifted. Whereas the majorities were once wholly

14

outside of the college and university system, they are now moving into it. This means that as never before they have an opportunity to become members of our elites. I go back to Thomas Jefferson, who in his famous exchange of letters with John Adams, said that the American democracy would not survive unless it could develop "an aristocracy of virtue and talent." It was Jefferson who said this—Jefferson the radical and the Jacobin, the Jefferson who hated the aristocracies of birth, privilege, and wealth in a Europe encrusted in the blood-rust of centuries. Yet this same Jefferson said that America would have to develop an aristocracy of virtue and talent. We no longer use the words *aristocracy* or *virtue;* let us call them creative minorities of character and ability.

I am not talking now of a meritocracy, which is a mechanical, wholly intellectual approach to the problem of the elite. I am talking of what is is potential within some of our best young carriers of promise. The qualitative task of the university has to do with them. There are two kinds of elites, of course, in every society. One is the *commanding* elite, which has to do with power and authority. The other is the *intellectual* or *creative* elite, which has to do with symbols, words, ideas, ideals, reforms, designs, colors, rhythms. The distinction between them ought not to be made too sharp; they intersect. One of the best instances of their intersection was President Kennedy. The reason he was so evocative a symbol to so many young people was that he spoke to them as a member of each of the elites with one foot in the commanding elite and one in the creative. Because of that he was able, for a time, to break down the hostility between these elites, a hostility which one finds through much of American and European history. Part of our task is to diminish some of that hostility, to develop some kind of hospitality between them, to see whether we can get our young people to understand that the tasks of government are not the tasks of corrupt or power-mad politicians, that they are in many ways the noblest tasks of our society. In a Periclean sense, they carry with them not only the decision-making process but the expression of the ethos of the society. We want to make sure that the young people who move into these elites do not break the roots they had in the soil of the mass society. Eugene Debs once said, "When I rise, I hope it will not be from my people but with them." I trust that our young university people, as they move into the commanding and creative elites, will remember this.

The cultural and educational explosions thus far have been horizontal, not vertical. That is to say, they have had to do with the further spread of what has already been thought and achieved in the human spirit, rather than with the deepening and further creativeness of the tradition. We need now to move beyond these horizontal explosions to the vertical revolution, to a creative America.

VI

This leads me to my fifth revolution—the *time revolution.* I want to develop some of the implications of the automation revolution in making more time available for more people in America. There have been leisure-class societies in the past—of Periclean Athens, Renaissance Venice and Florence, of Elizabethan England—in which the leisure of a few was made possible by the toil and exploitation of the many. What I see ahead in America is not another such leisure-class society, but a *leisure society.* By making available to more people—whether by cutting down the working day or week or by increasing vacations—it will be characterized by freedom from drudgery as the new dimension of freedom.

16

But this will not mean much unless we can rid ourselves of our sleazy attitudes toward "the job." There was a time when work meant something in the American ethos —a task that a man took pride in, that gave him a chance to express and fulfill himself. Instead of that, we now talk of the job. The job is something that we put as little of ourselves into as we can, that we try to get as much for as we can, and that we try to get away from as fast as we can. What we have done has been to replace the concept of work by the concept of the job. We shall not do much with the time revolution until we recapture the idea of the dignity and creativeness of work. It may be work on the job: a man able to find meaningful work on his job is one of the luckiest and happiest of men. But it may also mean new time released for work away from the job. There is a group of amateurs developing in our civilization (using *amateurs* in the quite literal sense of lovers) who love what they do, whether it is playing in a string quartet, or being a Civil War buff, or puttering away with carpentry in the basement or garage, or daubing away on canvas, or working within community organizations, or using volunteer time for teaching. We have an opportunity to become a nation of amateurs, finding meaningful work. This may perhaps bring the father back into the home, giving him an opportunity to share with his son and daughter some of the fruits of the reading revolution, the paperback revolution, the cultural explosion.

There is also the question of play, which is as important as work. We make a cult of fun. You go somewhere and they say, "Have fun." You come back and they say, "Did you have fun?" and you have to lie about it. You've got to have fun, even if it kills you. This is the fun imperative of our time. Fun may actually be high adventure, marvelously zany and recreating. But in our time it tends to be

17

nervous, tension-filled, frenetic. Here again, we need to recapture the idea of play—play as the full expressiveness of body, mind, and spirit, not in order to produce something (as with work) but for the sake of expressiveness itself.

Here I want to add one of the ironic paradoxes of our time. I spoke awhile ago of the leisure-class societies of Athens, Florence, and Elizabethan England. The leisure they gave to the few was provided by the work-driven many. In our time the one group unlikely to have much leisure, in the sense of time for play, work, amateurism, is the elite group—those in top positions of government, corporations, trade unions, universities and churches. Thus we have a rather elegant paradox—that in the leisure-class society the leisure of the few was provided by the work-driven many, but in our society the leisure of the many will very largely be provided by the work-driven few.

VII

The last of the revolutions is the *revolution of values*. The time revolution provides a chance not only for a new conception of work and play, but for a transvaluation of values. I included in my *America as a Civilization* a section on American life goals, in which I talked of the acknowledged goals of power, money, success, prestige, security, and happiness. There was a long review by the late Clyde Kluckhohn in *World Politics*, pointing out that perhaps the American revolutions had been moving too fast for me too. While those life goals were true four or five years before my book was published, said Kluckhohn, they were no longer true at the end of 1957. I am certain that if Professor Kluckhohn had lived he would say that they are even less true now, that new values are taking the place of these traditional power and money and

18

success-oriented values. It is certainly not true among the young people as a majority or the society as a total society, but it may be true of the creative marginal groups who are the value-carriers for university campuses. There is an opportunity for a transvaluation of value.

There is a story about Gertrude Stein, a somewhat eccentric American writer who lived most of her life in France. On her deathbed, in Paris, she turned to her friend Alice Toklas and asked, "Alice, what's the answer?" Alice looked at her sadly and said, "Gertrude, we just don't know." There was a long pause. Then Miss Stein asked, "Well then, Alice, what is the question?"

The test of a society in terms of its values hinges on the kind of questions that are asked in it—not just the overt questions, but the covert ones: not just the ones we teach and preach, but the ones we live. After one of my classes I said to a student, "Let's take a walk." We walked for an hour. I tried to convince him that, given his gifts, he ought to go into the Foreign Service, to put his gifts at the service of his country. At the end of the hour he asked me, "What's the precentage for me?" I knew then that there was a wall of non-communication between us.

In New York on the Avenue of the Americas, there are still some shops where you can buy novelty signs. I remember stopping at the window of one of these shops caught by a sign inside. It read: "If you are so smart, why aren't you rich?" That really got me. I stood for a long time looking at it, then in disgust I walked away. I hadn't walked more than a few blocks before I came back. I was like a chicken fascinated by a snake. I stood there again for a long time. Finally, with a sigh of relief, I walked away. I had the answer. The answer was that it was the wrong question—a question that assumed it was smart to be smart and wonderful to be rich.

We ask a good many wrong questions in our society.

19

Perhaps we are beginning to ask some of the right ones. Who am I? What are my connections with my family, my community, my country, with my fellow in humanity? Do I dare make the journey into the interior which is the most dangerous journey of all, and face what I find there? Do I have work that I care about? Am I capable of play, of giving and receiving love? Can I explore the depths and heights of joy? Do I dare face tragedy without being destroyed by it? Do I have a sense of natural universe, the carpet of the earth and, the tent of the sky, and the whole world of sight and sound and color? But most of all, do I have a sense of the human connection which ties me to other human beings, so that what happens to them happens to me?

Perhaps if we ask some of these questions, with the new time at our disposal, we may be able to carry through a values revolution, and make our civilization more credible to our young people. They may then stretch out their hands to claim the future. If we don't do this, then what Adlai Stevenson once said will prove true: there will be other and bloodier hands than ours that stretch out to that future to claim it.

REVOLUTION AND COUNTER-REVOLUTION— THE UNITED STATES AND CANADA

BY SEYMOUR MARTIN LIPSET

THE STRONG cultural similarity between English-speaking Canada and the United States has often led citizens of the latter to wonder why the two remain in separate polities. Yet, though these two nations probably resemble each other more than any other two nations on earth, there are consistent patterns of difference between them. To discover and analyze the factors which perpetuate such differences among nations is one of the more intriguing and difficult tasks in comparative study.

Any effort to specify the values, ethos, or national character of nations confronts the problem that such statements are necessarily made in a comparative context. Thus the assertion that the United States or Canada is a materialistic nation, that it is equalitarian, that its family system is unstable, obviously does not refer to these characteristics in any absolute sense. The statement that a national value system is equalitarian clearly does not imply the absence of severe differences in power, income, wealth, or status. Generally this statement means that from a comparative perspective, nations defined as equalitarian tend to place more emphasis on universalistic criteria in judging others, and tend to deemphasize the institutionalization of hierarchical differences. However, the key word here is comparative. No one suggests that any given complex social structure is in fact equalitarian in any absolute sense. The same may be said about the terms "aristocratic" and "ascriptive" when applied to complex modern societies. No society is in fact ascriptive in any total sense; all systems about which we have systematic empirical data reveal considerable social mobility, both up and down. What we are speaking of here are relative differences. Macroscopic sociology employs polarity concepts when it compares core aspects of societies—*gemeinschaft–gesellschaft,* organic solidarity–mechanical solidarity, inner-directed–other-directed, diffuseness–specificity, achievement–ascription, traditional–modern—and this approach purposely exaggerates such differences for analytic purposes.

One particularly effective schema for systematically classifying the central values of social systems is the pattern-variables as originally set forth by Talcott Parsons. These are dichotomous categories of modes of interaction. Those distinctions which seem particularly suitable for the analysis of the United States and Canada are achievement–ascription, universalism–particularism, self-orientation–collectivity-orientation, and equalitarianism–elitism. (The latter is not one of Parsons' distinctions, but one added here.) A society's value system may emphasize that a person in his orientation to others: 1) treats them in terms of their abilities and performances or in terms of inherited qualities (achievement–ascription) ; 2) applies a general standard or responds to some personal attribute or relationship (universalism–particularism) ; 3) perceives the separate needs of others or subordinates the individual's needs to the interests of the larger group (self-orientation–collectivity-orientation) ; and 4) stresses that all persons must be respected because they are human beings or emphasizes the general superiority of those who hold elite positions (equalitarianism–elitism) .[1]

The great mass of literature on these two North American democracies suggests the United States to be more achievement-oriented, universalistic, equalitarian, and self-oriented than Canada. Previous tentative evaluations of all the major English-speaking nations indicated that Canada is very much like the United States on these value dimensions, that both lie somewhere between the other two Anglo-American societies, Great Britain and Australia.[2] Since the value differences between Canada and the United States are not great, we expect to find strong similarities in many social characteristics, such as the demographic profile, occupational structures, and various institutional arrangements, e.g., labor-management relationships. The test of the utility of the comparative approach to the two North American societies so similar in value orientations depends upon specifying the special differences that *do* exist and identifying the historic issues and problems which sustain the near-differences between them.

Though many factors in the history of these nations have determined the current variations between them, these particular factors may be singled out: the varying origins of their political systems and national identities, varying religious traditions, and different frontier experiences. In general terms, the value orientations in English-speaking Canada stem from a counter-revolutionary past, a continuing need to differentiate itself from the United States, the influence of monarchial institutions, a dominant Anglican religious tradition, and a less individualistic and more governmentally controlled frontier expansion than was present on the American frontier.

II

Both nations are largely urbanized, heavily industrialized, and politically stable. They share many of the same ecological and demographic conditions, approximately the same level of economic development, and similar rates of

23

upward and downward social mobility. To a very great extent Canada and the United States share the same values, but as Kaspar Naegele has pointed out, in Canada these values are held much more tentatively.[3] Both are new peoples and new states, but Canada's relationship to Britain has helped perpetuate in a North American nation elements of a set of values having Old World origins and a conservative character. Thus, while equality and achievement are values emphasized in both North American societies, in Canada the emphasis is somewhat less and therefore the contrast between the nations remains one of degree.

Perhaps no other value emphases are as paramount in American life as the twin values of equalitarianism and achievement. Both have been strongest in the school system where the principles of the "common school," and "equal opportunity for success" remain viable educational ideals. In the United States the effective emphasis on achievement and on equality of opportunity is reflected by the demands of lower status individuals for access to education as a means to success, and the recognition by the privileged that education as a means to success must be given to all who are qualified. By contrast, in Canada education has had a more elitist and ascriptive import. These value differences are indicated by a comparison of college enrollment figures. In Canada only 9.2 percent of the 20–24-year-old age group compared to 30.2 percent in the United States were enrolled in institutions of higher learning in 1960. Even on the secondary school level, the United States shows a higher level of enrollment (76 percent) than Canada (64 percent).[4]

It has been suggested that elitist tendencies among Canadians account for the education of a limited few at the college level. Some Canadian writers have pointed out that until very recently education in their country

24

was designed to train an ecclesiastical and political elite much in the British tradition.[5] In Canada "only a small part of the youth was expected to attend the university; higher education was reserved for an intellectual elite— and for the children of the well-to-do."[6]

The content of the education curricula also appears to reflect value differences. In the United States, where status differences are seemingly less emphasized than in Canada, education curricula include more vocational, technical, and professional courses in "academic" type schools and colleges. This reflects the American view that education should not only be concerned with the transmission of intellectual and purely academic skills but should also provide practical knowledge that is directly applicable to an occupational situation.[7]

Canadian educators have shown resistance to the inclusion of purely vocational and professional curricula, especially in institutions of higher learning. Technical training has been viewed as corrupting the "aristocracy of intellect," those being educated for political and social leadership. Canadians, therefore, differ from Americans in being more eager to maintain the humanist emphasis in the curricula, a point of view which seems to accompany ascriptive values in other societies as well. So we find that Latin is still taught in most Canadian secondary schools.[8] The humanist tradition in Canadian education may be related also to the greater strength of traditional religion in Canada. But, as S. D. Clark notes, "the strength of the puritan tradition in Canadian society has not been unrelated to the strength of the aristocratic tradition. . . ."[9]

Education is one area in which there is some systematic comparative evidence concerning the varying opinions of Canadians and Americans. A survey of the attitudes of samples of educators and citizens sought to assess public perceptions of the task of education, and to discover the extent to which perceptions of Canadians and Americans diverge. Sixteen basic elements, synthesized from some of the most notable statements of school functions, made from the time of Horace Mann on, were classified into four mutually exclusive categories: intellectual dimensions, social dimensions, personal dimensions, and productive dimensions. The results point up the validity of many of the impressionistic generalizations such as those cited above concerning differences in national orientations. "The analysis of regional differences demonstrated that there were greater differences between Canada and any single American region than there were between any two American regions. Comparisons between all [English-speaking] Canadians and all Americans revealed even greater differences."[10]

The data indicate that "Canadians, as a group, assigned considerably higher priority than did Americans to knowledge, scholarly attitudes, creative skills, aesthetic appreciation and morality, as outcomes of schooling. Americans emphasized physical development, citizenship, patriotism, social skills and family living much more than did Canadians."[11] These findings that Americans are more likely than Canadians to view education as a means of gaining facilities in interpersonal skills, while Canadians tend more to see schooling as a way of training youth in the traditional values and high culture of the society, are congruent with the assumption that Canada is more elitist than its neighbor. Elsewhere, I have elaborated the thesis that the great concern of Americans with getting along with others, as reported by many European observers over the past century and a half, is closely linked to its strong emphasis on egalitarianism. The very fact that claims to higher status are less stable in the United States than in countries with more elitist orientations has made Americans more sensitive to the opinions of others and seemingly more concerned with imparting social adjustment skills to their children.[12]

The results of this opinion survey support the idea presented in many analyses of Canadian education that the country is caught in a dilemma between European and American orientations.[13] There are many in Canada today who see a clash between quantity and equality, and who choose quality by explicitly defending an elitist national policy. One critic of the emphasis on equality in education writes that "In Canada . . . there seems no valid reason . . . why our educational aims should be cluttered with this awkward word [democracy]. We should stop being concerned about the common man and instead turn our attention to the aristocratic elite upon whom the quality of our civilization depends."[14] Conversely Canadian educators who favor equalitarianism complain that Canadians are too traditional, that they see amount of knowledge gained and intellectual discipline as the only measures of education.[15]

Status distinctions, which exist in all nations, have less legitimacy in the United States than they do in Canada. The Canadian sociologist Kaspar Naegele concluded that the evidence on the subject indicates there is "less emphasis in Canada on equality than there is in the United States" and "a greater acceptance of *limitation,* of hierarchical patterns."[16] For example, the greater strength of elitist and ascriptive value emphases in Canada would seem to be reflected in the paternalistic organization of the family, in the reverence paid to the clergy by the laity, in the diffuse deference granted the old by the young, men by women, teachers by students, and politicians by the electorate.[17] From James Bryce to S. D. Clark, sociological oriented observers have stressed the greater respect for political leaders in Canada than in the United States, symbolized in part by Canadian loyalty to mon-

27

archical institutions. W. L. Morton has pointed out that among the institutions and norms linked to monarchy and cabinet government has been:

. . . the limited franchise and the idea that the franchise was a trust. Another was the British system of justice, challenged at the time by the principle of election applied to the selection of judges by the Jacksonian Democrats across the border. Yet another was the sense of public rank and personal honor. . . . The monarchy, in short, subsumed a heterogeneous and conservative society governed in freedom under law, law upheld by monarchy, where the republic would have levelled the diversities and made uniform the various groups by breaking them down into individuals, free indeed, but bound by social conformity and regimented by an inherent social intolerance.[18]

It is significant that Canadian political debates concerning the suffrage in the late nineteenth century still involved discussions of how much property a man should have to qualify to vote. Manhood suffrage was not enacted federally until 1898.[19] In the United States, the equalitarian emphasis facilitated the extension of male suffrage among whites almost everywhere by 1845.[20]

The American populist and equalitarian ethos also "leads to certain impatience with legal process and, occasionally, to outright disrespect for law."[21] There are several indicators of the differences in Canadian and American respect for public authority. Where diffuse respect for public authority exists, we should expect to find greater reliance on informal social controls based on traditional obligations. One indicator of the relative strength of the informal normative mechanisms of social control as compared with the restrictive emphases of legal sanctions may be the extent to which a nation requires police protection or lawyers. The data in Table 1 indicate that the United States ratio of police to population is more than one-third greater than that of Canada, a difference that holds for communities of the same size. The proportionately fewer lawyers in private practice in Canada (one for 1,630 people) as compared to the United States (one of 868) points to the much lower propensity of Canadians to rely on the law, even for civil matters.[22]

TABLE 1

Number and Rates of Police Protection in
Canada and the United States

Country	Number of Police Personnel	Ratio per 100,000 Population
CANADA (1961)	26,189	143.2
UNITED STATES (1962)	360,000	193.8

Source: Canada: Dominion Bureau of Statistics, *Police Administration Statistics*, 1961, p. 18; United States: U. S. Department of Commerce, Bureau of the Census, *Statistical Abstract of the United States*, 1963, p. 436.

The greater obedience to the law by Canadians may be reflected also in varying crime rates in the two countries. Though data on crime rates are far from amenable to accurate cross-national comparisons, both countries offer the same definition and report statistics for several major criminal offenses. Perhaps the most dramatic such difference is that only one police officer in Canada was killed by criminal action while on duty, compared to 37 killed in the United States in 1961. By 1963, the United States figure had risen to 55 police officers killed in a single year, while the figure in Canada remained at one.[23] (The United States has about ten times the population of Canada.) The data in Table 2 indicate that United States crime rates for various offenses are substantially higher than Canadian rates for the same offenses.

It is therefore not at all surprising, as one writer has remarked, that "Canadians are today perhaps more aware of the differences in their attitudes toward the law than anything else distinguishing them from Americans."[24] Half a century ago, James Bryce suggested that this habit of obedience to the law among Canadians "was formed

TABLE B

Adults Charged on Selected Indictable Offenses, by Class of Offense, 1960, for Canada and the United States

| | CANADA | | UNITED STATES* | |
	Number	Rate per 100,000 Pop.	Number	Rate per 100,000 Pop.
Criminal Homicide	207	1.2	7,956	7.3
Burglary	8,267	46.4	137,800	126.7
Forgery and Counterfeiting	1,158	6.4	25,244	23.2
Fraud and Embezzlement	2,414	13.5	42,189	38.8
Theft-Larceny	15,545	87.2	237,193	218.1

Source: Canada: Dominion Bureau of Statistics, *Canada Year Book,* 1962, p. 356; United States: U.S. Bureau of Census, *Statistical Abstracts of the United States,* 1962, p. 152.

* The rates for the U.S. were computed from a total population base of 108,779,000; for Canada's rates, the population base used was 17,814,000. The weaker authority of the American federal government as compared to the Canadian over local policing makes it more difficult for the former to collect reliable crime statistics; hence the discrepancy in the proportion of the total population for whom data exist.

under governments that were in those days monarchical in fact as well as in name, and it has persisted. . . . The sentiment of deference to legal authority, planted deep in days when that authority was regarded with awe as having an almost sacred sanction, has lived on into a time when the awe and sacredness have departed. . . ."[25]

Many have argued that the more widespread deferential respect for the elite in Canada as compared with the United States, rather than a more libertarian popular opinion, underlies the freedom of political dissent and guaranteed civil liberties so characteristic of English-speaking Canada. The emphasis on diffuseness and elitism in the Canadian system is reflected in the ability of the more unified and influential elites to control the system so as to inhibit the emergence of populist movements, such as McCarthyism, which express political intolerance. However, as S. D. Clark warns, McCarthyism (like Coughlinism and the Ku Klux Klan) does not indicate greater intolerance in the United States as compared to Canada so much as it reflects the strength of populist, anti-elitist values:

The attack of Joseph McCarthy upon Communist influences in the government of the United States is a clear and genuine expression of the American frontier, isolationist spirit. . . . In Canada it would be hard to conceive of a state of political freedom great enough to permit the kind of attacks upon responsible leaders of the government which have been carried out in the United States. More careful examination of the American community in general, and perhaps of the academic community in particular, would probably reveal that, in spite of the witch hunts in that country, the people of the United States enjoy in fact a much greater degree of freedom than do the people of Canada.[26]

Ironically, civil liberties for unpopular groups would seem to be stronger in elitist democracies than in egalitarian ones. The lesser respect for public authorities in the United States than in Canada may also be indicated by the considerable variation in the extent to which the public has insisted on the right to elect officials or to change them with the fortunes of elections.[27] In Canada legal officers tend to have life tenure, and are not directly involved in politics. Judges in Canada at every level are appointed for life by the federal authorities. Crown-Attorneys are designated by the provincial governments

31

for indefinite terms, and are rarely terminated before retirement. They are not fired when a new party comes to power, and since prohibited from political activity, they are never under pressure to handle cases in a way that might facilitate their re-election or attainment of higher electoral office.[28]

In the United States not only are more legal offices open to election, but elections are more frequent than in any other modern society. In a recent discussion of American urban politics, Edward Banfield and James Wilson point out that "our government [in the United States] is permeated with politics. This is because our constitutional structure and our traditions afford individuals manifold opportunities not only to bring their special interests to the attention of public officials but also—and this is the important thing—to compel officials to bargain and to make compromises . . . there is virtually no sphere of 'administration' apart from politics."[29] Such a comment underlines the populist sentiments and structures that pervade the American polity. The strong equalitarian emphasis in the United States which presses for expression in the *vox populi* makes Americans more derisive and critical of their politicians and government bureaucrats.

The same differentiating factors seemingly are reflected in varying administrative practices at the national government level. Alexander Brady, a prominent Canadian student of comparative political institutions, has strongly emphasized these differences:

In Ottawa, no less than in London, the dividing line between the politician craving publicity and the permanent official cherishing anonymity is drawn higher in the administrative hierarchy than in Washington. A political party replacing another in power does not, as in the United States, introduce to public office a new and large retinue of top advisors and administrators. It assumes that in the civil service it will find a reliable and competent corps of officials to supplement its thinking and implement its decisions. The deputy-minister as the permanent chief of a department is a non-political figure who normally brings to the aid of his minister the resources of seasoned experience and knowledge.[30]

The lesser respect for the law, for the "rules of the game" in the United States, may be viewed as inherent in a system in which equalitarianism is strongly valued and in which diffuse elitism is lacking. Generalized deference is not accorded to those at the top; therefore, in the United States there is a greater propensity to redefine the rules or to ignore them. The legitimacy and decisions of the leadership are constantly being questioned. While Canadians incline toward the use of "lawful" and traditionally institutionalized means for altering regulations which they believe are unjust, Americans seem more disposed to employ informal and often extralegal means to correct what they perceive as wrong.

The greater lawlessness and corruption in the United States may be attributed in part to the greater strength of the achievement and self-orientation values in the more populous nation. As Robert Merton has pointed out, a strong emphasis on achievement means that "the moral mandate to achieve success thus exerts pressure to succeed, by fair means if possible and by foul means if necessary."[31] Merton accounts for the greater adherence to approved means of behavior in much of Europe compared to the United States as derivative from variations in the emphasis on achievement for all. And the same logic implies that since Americans are more likely than their Canadian neighbors to be concerned with the achievement of ends—particularly pecuniary success—that they will be less concerned with the use of the socially appropriate *means*; hence we should expect a higher incidence of deviations from conventional norms in politics and other aspects of life south of the 49th parallel.[32]

The variations in the legal status of labor conflict and the behavior of the trade unions in the two countries illustrate both the greater willingness of Americans to accept conflict as a "normal" method of resolving disputes and to violate rules and laws to attain desired ends. Thus in Canada a union's right to strike must be earned through a process of legal certification of majority backing (a restriction which does not exist in the United States where any group of workers may employ the strike weapon in order to resolve a dispute).[33] And where labor conflicts have occurred, "there has generally been less violent conflict between workers and employers [in Canada than in the United States]. The use of professional strikebreakers, labor spies, 'goon squads,' 'vigilante' groups, armed militia, and other spectacular features of industrial warfare in the United States in previous decades have been absent from the Canadian scene—again with several notable exceptions."[34]

The greater diffidence of Canadians with respect to their adherence to achievement and self-orientation values may also be reflected in their reluctance to be over-optimistic, assertive, or experimentally inclined in economic affairs. This Canadian caution manifests itself in several ways: one is "that Canadians take out more insurance *per capita* than any other race in the world. Another is that they buy considerably less on hire-purchase [installment plan] than the Americans. . . . The average Canadian is also cautious about his savings, favouring Government bonds and savings banks. Whereas over the years the American big investor has tended to take a risk on the future of Canada and invest heavily in more speculative Canadian enterprises, the wealthy Canadian cautiously puts his money into Standard Oil of New Jersey."[35]

The earliest empirical efforts to determine Canadian self-perceptions, made in the thirties, indicate that Canadians of that period thought of themselves as "quieter, slower in tempo, and saner in quality" than Americans, saw Americans as loud, shrewd, less honest, and more anxious to get rich quickly.[36] Clearly, as Canadian sociologists Kaspar Naegele and Dennis Wrong have argued, the Horatio Alger success story has never taken hold in Canadian society, perhaps due to Canadian resistance to economic aggressiveness, social informality, and unabashed materialism.[37] Canadian historian Arthur Lower has even argued that "Henry Ford was a figure who could hardly have been other than American. Canada did not provide a stage for such as he. Yet this was not on account of lack of opportunities here [in Canada] for accumulating wealth, but rather because that process called for more betting on the sure thing than was necessary across the border."[38]

The variation in the strength of the achievement and self-orientation values in the United States and Canada may account for another political difference—the fact that "free enterprise" ideology, though accepted in Canada, has never been the source of as violent political conflicts there as in the United States. The greater respect for government and political leaders, derived in part from elitism and in part from the need dictated by special historic circumstances (see below) requiring that the central government intervene repeatedly in economic and local political matters to assure national survival, has inhibited the development of strong economic individualism as a dominant political virtue. As James Bryce remarked some decades ago, "the policy of *laissez-faire* has few adherents in a country which finds in governmental action or financial support to private enterprise the quickest means of carrying out every promising project. So when

35

party conflicts arise over these matters, it is not the principle that is contested . . . but the plan advocated by the Government or the Opposition as the case may be."[39]

Canada has clearly been much more collectivity-oriented than the United States. In recent years, proposals for medicare, grants for large families, government intervention in the economy, and public ownership of major enterprises have encountered much less opposition north of the border than south of it. "The extreme economic individualism expressed by such slogans as 'the best government is the one that governs least' does not have such deep roots in Canada" as it has in the United States.[40] As one English writer notes: "One of the strange contradictions of Canada is that although it has never had anything resembling a Socialist Government in Ottawa, the list of its 'nationalized' industries is almost as imposing as Britain's: more than half the railways; the principal airline; most of radio and television; the Atomic Energy Corporation and one of the biggest uranium producers; a big plastics industry; many of the power utilities [and telephone and telegraph]; and the entire liquor retailing business."[41] And as a Canadian points out, "it is interesting to note that at a time when the *laissez-faire* philosophy was prevailing in the rest of the Western World, there was no protest in Canada against government intervention and interference, not even from business circles."[42] Far from turning to McCarthyism or Goldwaterism, Canadian conservatives responded to years of political defeat by renaming their party the *Progressive* Conservatives.

The emphases on achievement and self-orientation in the United States are strongly linked to universalism. In the United States there is a proclaimed need to treat everyone according to the same standard. This universalistic objective underlies the concept of the "melting pot" which holds that no one should be disqualified from full

36

participation on the grounds of ethnic origin or other social distinctions. The melting pot concept is the achievement-orientation applied to entire ethnic groups.[43] In contradistinction to the melting pot of the United States, Canadians speak of their society as a "mosaic," a concept which enunciates in theory the "right to sustained collective individuality."[44] As Canadian sociologist John Porter points out, the difference between the ideas of the *melting pot* and the *mosaic* is "one of the principal distinguishing features of United States and Canadian society at the level of social psychology as well as that of social structure."[45] Vincent Massey, former Governor-General, has expressed the Canadian stress on the presentation of particularistic values: "We have been successful in our manner of adjusting the relations of the varied communities making Canada their home. About one out of three speaks French as his mother tongue. He is no minority assimilated within a common Canadianism, but rather a partner sharing equally in the joint project of Confederation. Then there are the 'new Canadians' of whom two million from Great Britain and from Europe have reached our shores since 1945. . . . We try to fit in the newcomers much as they are, as pieces in the Canadian mosaic."[46] Canadians emphasize the contribution which diverse ethnic and linguistic groups bring to Canadian life in the form of cultural heritage. "New Canadians have been encouraged to maintain many of their distinctive folk traditions, and their songs, dress, and folklore," and they "are often publicized as indications of the richness and diversity of Canadian life—an approach to ethnic differences that is much less common in the United States. . . ."[47]

Canadian particularism has been demonstrated also in the requirement, in existence until recently, that Canadian passports indicate ethnic origin, e.g., a Canadian of German origin even though the German origin may go back more than a century. The Canadian Census not only differs from the American in that it records religious data gathered from each individual, but it also reports on the national origins of every Canadian, except for Jews. The latter, regardless of country of paternal ancestry, are classified as Jews in the category of national origin as well as religion.

Canada's political party system has witnessed the rise of a number of "particularistic" third parties, various French Canadian nationalist or separatist movements, plus the Progressives, Social Credit, and the Cooperative Commonwealth Federation (CCF). The last, a socialist party, has recently joined with the Canadian Labor Congress to form the trade-union based New Democratic Party, the largest contemporary "third" party. This pattern of Canadian politics—i.e. the continued presence of strong particularistic third parties—is consistent with the assumption that Canada is more particularistic (group attribute conscious) than the seemingly more universalistic United States.

III

Many writers seeking to account for value differences between the United States and Canada suggest that they stem in large part from the revolutionary origins of the United States and the counter-revolutionary history of Canada, from two disparate founding ethos. The Loyalist émigrés from the American Revolution and Canada's subsequent repeatedly aroused fears of United States encroachment fostered the institutionalization of a counter-revolutionary or conservative ethos.[48] By contrast the core values of the United States, linked to the idealistic ideology which emerged during the Revolution, were codified in the Declaration of Independence and elaborated in the

principles successfully pressed by the Jeffersonian Democrats in the formative post-Revolutionary decades.

In these counter-revolutionary beginnings of Canada,
we find the clue to the continuance of British ascriptive
and elitist value patterns. The Canadian historian Arthur
Lower has pointed out that "in its new wilderness home
and its new aspect of British North Americanism, colonial
Toryism made its second attempt to erect on American soil
a copy of the English social edifice. From one point of
view this is the most significant thing about the Loyalist
movement; it withdrew a class concept of life from the
south, moved it up north and gave it a second chance."[49]

During the American Revolution, Nova Scotia had a
population of 17,000; almost double that number of Loyalists entered it afterwards, "swallowing the older 'neutral
Yankee' elements in an ardently Loyalist mass." New
Brunswick was set up as a separate province in 1784,
largely because of the great Loyalist influx. The Loyalist
settlers in Upper Canada (now Ontario) "would form
the backbone of western resistance in a second war with
the United States, the War of 1812. They were the original
founders of the present province of Ontario, and did
much to mould its character. On one hand, they brought
to Canada a conservative outlook, a quick distrust of any
new idea that might be called republican, and a readiness
to make loyalty the test for almost everything. On the
other, they themselves represented a declaration of independence against the United States, a determination to
live apart from that country in North America."[50] Thus
Tory conservatism and anti-Americanism affected "not
only the St. John Valley where the loyalists were a majority, but other regions where they were a minority."
These "interlocked neatly with the prevalent conceptions
of oligarchy and privilege."[51]

After the Revolution, undisguised efforts were made to

check American influences. The first governors, Simcoe and Carleton, of what is now Ontario and Quebec were men who had played a leading role in fighting the Revolution. To them republican principles were anathema.[52] The anti-revolutionary and anti-American character of Canada's political and social development helped strengthen ethnic particularism and ecclesiasticism. The English Protestant rulers of French Canada opposed assimilation and weakening of the semi-Establishment status of the Catholic church in Quebec as a means of resisting Americanization. Sir Robert Falconer says that "as late as 1822 Lord Dalhousie favored the French Canadians of the lower province as a means of make-weight against Americanizing tendencies which he discerned in Upper Canada."[53] Support for the hierarchically organized churches, Anglican and Roman, served to reinforce hierarchical, anti-democratic tendencies. As the famed Canadian historian Harold Innis noted, a "counter-revolutionary tradition implies an emphasis on ecclesiasticism."[54]

Continued Canadian allegiance to the British monarchy undoubtedly has also contributed to the greater sense of legitimacy for hierarchical distinctions characteristic of the northern nation. In the early history of Canada, the public authorities tried consciously to foster such values as a barrier to American influences.[55] Clark says: "Efforts to strengthen the political ties of Empire or of nation led to deliberate attempts, through land grants and political preferments, to create and strengthen an aristocracy in the colonies . . . and later in a less obvious fashion, in the Canadian nation. The democratic movement it was felt was liable to draw Canadian people closer to their neighbors to the south; and a privileged upper class was a bulwark of loyalty and conservatism."[56]

The unification of the British North American colonies into a federal union was procured by Empire-oriented

Canadian Conservatives who feared United States expansion across the border, and the growth in influence within Canada of reform-minded "pro-American" frontier settlers who favored local autonomy. The decision to provide Canada with a strong central government, which unlike that of the United States would be able to veto or "disallow" provincial laws, was designed to resist the democratic threat within and across the border.[57] According to W. L. Morton, "With the Reformers committed to local democracy, and the Conservatives to continental expansionism, it is not surprising that Confederation was, by and large, a Conservative party measure, and also a measure conservative in tone and substance. A striking venture in federalism, it neither, except in establishing representation by population, widened the basis of self-government nor altered the depository of sovereignty."[58]

In contrast to Canada, the United States is the result of a successful revolution and prolonged war of independence organized around the ideology embodied in the Declaration of Independence, which proclaimed the validity of equalitarian and universalistic social relations. Out of a sort of Utopian conception of men's equalitarian and universalistic relations with one another a national consciousness arose which infused men with a new awareness and new confidence in what they were and in their own kind.[59] The new value consensus and normative prescriptions of the American people were sustained by at least two major conditions: territorial expansion and nonalignment with European nations.

In newly independent societies there has often been a transition from a system dominated by traditionalist, usually aristocratic, values to one characterized by egalitarian concepts. Consequently, most struggles for independence have employed leftist ideologies—socialism today, and equality in revolutionary America—in which

41

man's status is to depend not upon inherited but achieved qualities. Thus the system in America was geared to abolish all forms of privilege and primogeniture and to reward achievement.

Despite the conviction of many revolutionary leaders that the struggle for independence was primarily an issue of political and national independence, large segments of the American people organized against the emergence of any ruling oligarchical forces. Many insisted that the franchise be extended to everyone, that the people be regarded as the source of power and authority. The very early arguments for the extension of the suffrage to all were "based on the rights of man given special impetus by the Declaration of Independence and the terms of conflict of the American Revolution."[60] The demands on American politicians to be competent and to deliver some rewards to the people were as natural in the revolutionary era as they are today. Although the Federalists attempted to preserve some elements of elitist values and resisted populist reforms, there is general agreement among historians that a major cause of their decline was the refusal to accommodate themselves to the strength of egalitarian sentiments. All succeeding parties were to be egalitarian in ideology and populist in spirit.[61]

The significance of the "leftist" egalitarian populist character of core values in the American political tradition may best be perceived from the vantage point of comparative North American history. For though American historians and political philosophers may debate the extent of radicalism, liberalism, leftism, or even conservatism, in Revolutionary and post-colonial American politics, there is little doubt in the mind of most Canadian historians. Looking at the divergent political history north and south of the border, they see the continued politics of their nation as reflecting the fact that it is the descendant of a counter-revolution, while the United States is the product of a successful revolution. Once these events had formed the structure of the two nations, their institutional characters were set. Subsequent events tended to enforce "leftist" values in the south, and "rightist" ones in the north. The success of the revolutionary ideology, the defeat of the Tories, and the emigration of many of them north to Canada or across the ocean to Britain—all served to enhance the strength of the forces favoring egalitarian democratic principles in the new nation and to weaken conservative tendencies. On the other hand, the failure of Canada to have a revolution of its own, the immigration of conservative elements, and the emigration of radical ones— all contributed to making Canada a more conservative and more rigidly stratified society. This does not mean, as S. D. Clark has pointed out, "that revolutionary forces developed no strength in Canada. We have had our revolutions but they have been largely unsuccessful, and being unsuccessful we try to forget them. Thus we have tended to dismiss our rebels of the past as misguided individuals out of accord with their fellow Canadians. . . ."[62]

American Democratic party reformers from Jackson to Bryan to Wilson to the leaders of the modern New Deal–Fair Deal–New Frontier–Great Society party have presented their programs as means of implementing the egalitarian ideals of the Revolution. In Canada, which not only emerged out of a defeated democratic revolution, but has a history of defeated nineteenth century reformist movements, advocates of progressive reforms can not link these to historic national movements. Of course, "as in other industrial societies, there has been some extension of social rights . . . [but] their haphazard development has come about more by the 'demonstration effect' of their existence in other countries, than because they have formed the social philosophy of either of the two parties which have been in power at the federal level."[63]

In addition to fostering politically relevant norms, American values have encouraged egalitarian social relations by contributing to the enormous increase in national wealth, an increase which made it possible to assure the lower classes a standard of living which would support their claim for equal treatment by those who excelled them in economic and political power. American values have engendered strong positive orientations toward hard work and economic development. The emphasis on equality and achievement reinforced the belief that one could and should get ahead by hard continuous work, frugality, self-discipline, and individual initiative. The absence of an aristocratic stratum following the Revolution left the United States free to develop a socially as well as economically dominant class of merchants and manufacturers whose desire for wealth was uninhibited by norms denigrating hard work and the accumulation of capital. Such norms were present in much of Europe, and to some extent even in Canada, although more among the French than the English. Thus the rapidity of American economic growth must be credited, in some degree, to a symbiotic relationship between economic motivation and the system of general values.

IV

The differences between American and Canadian religion have been of considerable significance in producing the admittedly small differences between the values of the two countries, as well as affecting national differences in political and economic development. Denominational religion, often evangelistic, secular, and voluntary in character, has contributed to the American emphases on self-orientation, egalitarianism, universalism, and achievement.

Conversely, religion in Canada retained its ecclesiastic character and its strong relationship to the state with the consequence that religious organization in Canada, emphasizing elitism and particularism, acted as a counterforce inhibiting excessive individualism (self-orientation) and egalitarianism.

In the first half century of the American Republic, the champions of religious traditionalism were seriously weakened, as the various state churches—Anglican in the South and Congregationalist in New England—were gradually disestablished. From the beginning, the United States was heir to a Calvinistic Puritanism which was stronger in the colonies than in the mother country, and it was congenial to modernity in a sense that the Anglican Church in English Canada and the Gallican Church in Quebec were not. The two denominations, Methodist and Baptist, which became dominant in the early nineteenth century, stressed religious doctrines that supported "antiaristocratic tendencies."[64] After the Revolution, the Calvinist doctrine with its belief in innate predestination was gradually supplanted by Arminian religious beliefs, not only as an evangelical revivalistic religion, but as a reflection of the fact that "in a period when special privileges of individuals were being called into question or being destroyed, there would naturally be less favor for that form of theology which was dominated by the doctrine of especial election of a part of mankind, a growing favor for forms which seemed more distinctly to be based upon the idea of the natural equality of all men."[65]

The Arminian emphasis on the personal attainment of grace, embodied in "doctrines of free will, free grace, and unlimited hope for the conversion of all men," even more than Calvinism, served as a religious counterpart to the democratic goals of equality and achievement.[66] A devout man was an ambitious man, and as Philip Schaff,

45

a Swiss theologian who eventually emigrated to America, reported, the "acquisition of riches is to them [the Americans] only a help toward higher spiritual and moral ends."[67] Righteousness was to be rewarded both in this life and in the hereafter.

The abolition of established religion in the United States fostered a strong commitment to voluntarism. This commitment, together with the considerable strength of the dissenting and anti-statist Methodist and Baptist denominations, meant that religion not only contributed to the economic orientations of the people, but also reinforced the egalitarian and democratic social ethos. Tocqueville pointed out that all American denominations were minorities and hence had an interest in liberty and a weak state. As he put it in discussing Catholics: "They constitute a minority, and all rights must be respected in order to assure to them the free exercise of their own privileges. These . . . causes induce them, even unconsciously, to adopt political doctrines which they would perhaps support with less zeal if they were preponderant."[68] Denominational voluntaristic religion not only reinforced the support for minority rights in the religious sphere, but also found deeply religious men in government arguing strongly that the rights of the irreligious and of Jews must be the same as those of Christians.[69]

In Canada state-related religion has provided that country with a hierarchical and traditionally rooted control mechanism that is largely lacking in United States history. Because of the strong tie between church and state in Canada, religious development there, in contrast to religious movements in the United States, has been less prone to both fundamentalism and experimentalism.

Both the Church of England and the Roman Catholic Church, which were hierarchically organized and received overt governmental support, gave strong suport to the established political and social order. Hence one found mutually reinforcing conservative forces at the summits of the class, church, and political structures.[70]

The interlocking character of political and religious conservatism may be seen in the extent to which patterns of marriage and divorce have been affected by religious practices. As recently as World War II, the law of most provinces, including Ontario, did not provide for civil marriage.[71] The extent to which Canadian religion has been more successful than American in maintaining traditional and conservative principles may be seen in the much lower divorce rate in Canada as compared with the United States, as shown in Table 3. The greater moral

TABLE 3

Divorce Rates per 1,000 Marriages for Specified
Years in Canada and the United States

Year	Canada	United States
1891	less than 1	60.0
1911	less than 1	93.4
1941	29.3	168.5
1951	41.0	230.4
1956	45.2	233.0
1960	53.5	257.3

Source: Canada: Dominion Bureau of Statistics, *Canada Year Book,* 1962, pp. 209, 211; United States: U. S. Department of Commerce, Bureau of the Census, *Statistical Abstracts of the United States,* 1962, p. 52, and United Nations, *Demographic Yearbook,* 1960 (New York), p. 607. See also Lincoln Day, "Patterns of Divorce in Australia and the United States," *American Sociological Review,* 29 (August 1964), pp. 509-22, esp. Table 2.

conservatism of English Canada is also revealed in the fact that many "blue laws" and Sunday observance regulations remained in force much longer to the north than the south, and, in fact, a number of such restrictions on behavior still exist in many Canadian cities.

The ecclesiastical character of the predominant Canadian religions have also greatly inhibited the development of egalitarian and achievement emphases comparable to those fostered by anti-elitist sects and denominations in the United States. American Protestantism, with its emphasis on the personal attainment of grace, reinforced the stress on personal achievement dominant in the secular value system. Both sets of values stressed individual responsibility, both rejected hereditary status. The Methodists and Baptists, who together contained the great majority of American Protestants, stressed religious doctrines that reinforced "anti-aristocratic tendencies."[72] In English Canada, the Anglican Church "set a standard of dignity for all the leading denominations which was absent in the United States."[73]

And while the dominant Arminian denominations have fostered economic ambition in the United States, Canadian ecclesiasticism has been less able to provide a stimulus for new forms of economic enterprise.

Religion has given support to an attitude of mind, and a governmental policy, which has placed a check upon that kind of economic and social mobility conducive to the development of capitalism. Churches are essentially status institutions, and this has meant that the organization of religion has served to maintain status distinctions that have had no meaning in terms of economic endeavor. The strength of the aristocratic tradition in Canada owes much to the influence of religion. . . . In English-speaking Canada . . . Church establishment in colonial times placed a considerable dependence upon a close alliance with a privileged upper class that lacked the imagination or inclination to take any sort of lead in the economic development of the country, and, although the formal disestablishment of the church weakened the religious support of such a class system, the organization of religion has continued to be sufficiently powerful to maintain to some degree the status distinctions of a religiously oriented rather than economically oriented society.[74]

Religious sects have, of course, developed in Canada, facilitated by much the same social conditions inherent in rapid social change as in the United States, i.e. the heavy shift of population to the frontier or the growing cities and the related social mobility, which have torn individuals from their traditional ties and made them available for recruitment to new loyalties. However, the fact that religion is less explicitly separated from the "national community" in Canada has meant that sects have been less able to survive there than in the United States. In Canada: "Political pressures," says Clark, "have forced the community to come to the support of organized religion and such support has placed a definite limitation upon sectarian activity. With the collective weight of the community brought to bear upon them, the sects have been forced to retreat behind a wall of isolation or build themselves into an integral part of the community, or else to seek denominational support by aligning themselves with the state and with the traditional institutions of the community."[75] Once the historic sects allied themselves with the established institutions in the community, their differences became less important and they found it easier to forget about sectarian differences and unite. As a result the union of the major "non-conformist" Protestant denominations proceeded much more rapidly in Canada than in the United States. The United Church of Canada was formed in 1925 out of a merger of Methodist, Presbyterian, and Congregationalist denominations. In many parts of English Canada, it now shares an unofficial but real "establishment" status with the Anglican church.[76]

V

Some of the flavor of the social distinctions in Canada and the United States which reflect the greater strength

49

of traditionalist and conservative values in the former, may be traced also to a Canadian frontier fashioned in a spirit of cautious defensiveness against American absorptionist tendencies. Since Canada felt that it had to be on constant guard against American expansionism, it could not afford to leave its frontier communities unprotected or autonomous. "It was the established tradition of British North America that the power of the civil authority should operate well in advance of the spread of settlement."[77] Law and order in the form of the centrally controlled Northwest Mounted Police moved into the frontier settlements before and along with the settlers. This contributed to the establishment of a greater tradition of respect for institutions of law and order on the Canadian frontier as compared with the American.

This famous force [Mounted Police] was organized in 1874. To the 300 men who composed it was given the task of seeing that the law was obeyed from Manitoba to the Rockies and from the forty-ninth parallel to the Artic Circle. . . . Organized whiskey traffic with the Indians was broken up within a year. Horse stealing was made so precarious that there was seldom need for the drastic community action which was the normal procedure in many parts of the American West. Perhaps most important of all, Canada was enabled to avoid the series of desperate conflicts with the Indians which was necessary to clear the way for the final advance of settlement in the United States.[78]

The Canadians, being more prone to identify liberty and democracy with legal traditions and procedures than with populism, the right of the people to rule, or with the freedom of business and enterprise, have given equal juridicial rights to minority and ethnic groups, while in the United States debates over the position of minority groups have been at the root of Indian wars and of the Civil War. On the American frontier the quality of law

50

enforcement was often dependent on local police authority which reflected the values of the frontiersmen, including their prejudices against Indians and their lack of understanding for legal procedures incorporating the guarantee of due process. In Canada Indian chiefs "were impressed by the fact that, if Indians were punished for crimes against the whites, the whites were equally punished for outrages against the Indians. Their previous experience [with American whites] had taught them to appreciate such impartial justice."[79] The Queen's peace was maintained even in the mining camps, which were characteristically undisciplined in the United States. Conditions during the gold rush in British Columbia differed greatly from those in the American western mining frontier. There were no vigilantes or massacres of Indians.[80]

The presence of national governmental controls weakened the development of excessive individualism which expresses itself south of the border in a greater faith in the future and a greater willingness to risk capital, personal security, or reputation. The Canadian frontier experience did not undermine the traditional bases of authority; Canadians even on the frontier retained a more deeply internalized sense of obligation, of the need to conform to the rules even when there was no visible threat of coercion. As the Canadian historian Arthur Lower has put it: "We have always carried authority and a code along with us, no matter how far from 'the law' we have happened momentarily to be. . . . The result has been less non-conformity in Canadian life than in America, less experimentation, more acceptance of standards built up in the long history of the English-speaking race."[81]

The frontier settlers in both North American nations spawned important reformist movements. They tended to see themselves as exploited by the dominant economic and political power centered in the eastern cities. To a

51

considerable extent, those located at the farther reaches of the nation sought to free themselves from this control. "It was this insistence upon local autonomy, this separatist spirit, which was the dominant characteristic of those revolutionary or reform movements which grew up in the interior parts of the continent."[82] For Canada, frontier separatism was always a threat to the integrity of the nation, and often constituted a pro-American liberal response. The Canadian government consequently engaged in systematic actions to reduce frontier autonomy, to guarantee that national institutions and values would dominate on the frontier.[83] The American government, however, had no reason to fear that frontier movements would be a source of secessionism, or would lead to demands for incorporation by a foreign neighbor.

In the United States, frontier agricultural, ranching, and mining areas, uncontrolled for long periods by any central government or policing system, provided unlimited opportunities, and disposed settlers to use their own resources as they saw fit. And these rugged individualists, the cowboy, the frontiersman, and even the vigilante, not the uniformed disciplined Mountie, are the heroes of American western settlement. The frontiersman, on the other hand, has never been a figure for special glorification in Canadian literature as he has been in American. "Canadian writers and critics drew back in well-bred horror from the distasteful crudities of the frontier, and looked, more resolutely than ever, eastward across the Atlantic to the source of all good things."[84]

Geography also served to reinforce social factors in reducing the influence of the more democratic and egalitarian practices of the frontier on the rest of the country. The Canadian prairies, the provinces of Manitoba, Saskatchewan, and Alberta, were separated from the populous East by the Great Lakes and a one thousand mile, almost uninhabitable, rock shield which ran north of the lakes. These "provided an effective barrier to close and constant intercourse."[85] And these same geographic factors reinforced the need for systematic government intervention to assure communications, since private enterprise could not afford the great cost of bridging the gap between east and west. "[T]he colonization of the West, in Canada, was to a large extent a government enterprise and not a purely private venture as in the United States. . . . The central government owned the land, brought the people, mainly immigrants, provided directly or indirectly the transport system and made sure that wheat would move within Canada at low rates."[86]

The considerable involvement of the Canadian government in fostering economic development enhanced the emphasis on collectivity as distinct from self-orientation values discussed earlier. Whether Conservative or Liberal, leftist or rightist, Canadian political leaders have recognized that a sparsely settled country bordering on a wealthy, powerful, and attractive neighbor, must supply many services through governmental agencies which could be furnished by private enterprise in nations with more densely settled populations.[87]

VI

Born in a prolonged struggle for independence, the United States defined itself from its beginnings in ideological terms. As many writers have noted, Americanism is an ideology, a set of integrated beliefs defining the good society. Property relations apart, the social aspects of the doctrine of Americanism have a close resemblance to socialism. Both urge that men should treat each other as equals regardless of their differences in ability or position, and that all should have an equal opportunity to succeed.

53

With these social concepts has gone a belief in populist democracy, in the right of the people to govern and in the assumption that sovereignty rests in the people. For much of American history, autocratic and highly stratified societies have constituted a negative reference image. From its founding until World War I, the United States saw itself politically to the left of, and in opposition to, European monarchical and aristocratic reactionary regimes. Americans sympathized with democratic revolutionaries and nationalists fighting reactionaries and foreign rulers. Following World War I, the United States increasingly took on the role of the most powerful western *capitalist* nation, a role which led the left, Communist, socialist, and the nationalist movements of the underdeveloped and then largely colonial nations, to see the United States as the principal center of conservatism and the source of support for conservatism, traditionalism, and imperialism. The United States, however, has rejected a conception of itself as a conservative power. It still sees itself as a supporter of the struggle against reactionary tyranny in the Communist countries, and a proponent of progressive democratic and egalitarian reforms in the underdeveloped nations of Africa, Asia, and Latin America. There can be little doubt, however, that America's world activities as supporter of existing regimes against Communist and sometimes non-Communist revolutionary movements has undermined much of this image, even within its own borders.

Canadian national identity is clearly not bound up with the ideology of a successful revolution or a dramatic political movement. Rather, as we have seen, Canadian identity is the product of a victorious counter-revolution, and in a sense must justify its *raison d'être* by emphasizing the virtues of being separate from the United States. Frank Underhill has pointed out that Canadians are the world's oldest and continuing anti-Americans.[88] The Canadian sense of nationality has always felt itself threatened by the United States, physically in earlier days, and culturally and economically in more recent years. As S. D. Clark has put it: "Canadian national life can almost be said to take its rise in the negative will to resist absorption in the American Republic. It is largely about the United States as an object that the consciousness of Canadian national unity has grown up. . . ."[89]

From Confederation in 1867 on, Canadian political leaders and intellectuals have sought to locate Canadian superiority over the United States in its rejection of the crudities of a populist democracy and culture. As against the powerful American model, Canada has always emphasized its connection with and resemblance to Britain.[90] "[I]n the field of literature, one could argue that Canadian writers have been less responsive than the Australian to American influences. As between English and American influences, they have preferred the English. . . ."[91] Loyalty to the British Crown has been one effective means of arousing sentiment against American intervention and control. The social consequence of Canadian allegiance to a British monarch has been the acceptance of a national purpose based on the principle of the "indivisibility of the Commonwealth." As Vincent Massey has put it, "There are some people in Canada with strong nationalist feelings who think that their end could only be achieved through a republican form of government. There are, happily, very few persons with such views, and they are profoundly misguided in labouring under the delusion that as a republic we could remain an independent nation. We could not. The Crown-in-Parliament is the supreme symbol of our nationhood and our greatest defense against absorption into a continental state."[92]

There is at present extensive United States capital investment in Canada, high consumption of American goods, and wide circulation of American communication media. Many have rebelled against this penetration into Canadian life.[93] The Canadian nationalist points to such facts as proof of "domination" by the United States.[94]

Nationalism in English Canada has undergone some curious changes from the time when it represented a left-wing, often pro-United States protest against the Imperial connection, and the closed economic-political-ecclesiastical system sustained by this connection. Today it is often the left-winger who is most anti-American and pro-British. The more traditional form of Canadian nationalism would seem to continue in the French-Canadian protest movements with their anti-English and anti-establishment overtones directed at those within Canadian borders who represent English cultural, political, and economic domination. As English Canadians seek to isolate Canada from the United States, French-Canadians look for means to assure the safety of their culture surrounded by two hundred million English speakers. In a sense both English and French Canadians have similar objectives, to protect two tiny minority cultures from being absorbed by more powerful neighbors.[95]

The problem of changing Canadian and American identities is clearly linked to the broad topic of this paper, the nature and sources of the differences in values and institutions of the two North American democracies. In the past decades the world image of the United States has changed drastically. Relatively few in the rest of the world still see the United States in the idealistic terms with which it views itself. To the leaders of the underdeveloped and the Communist world, and to many in the developed world, including Canada as well, the United States is now the leading defender of conservative traditional social forms, and is governed from within by an oligarchy or power-elite. Many Canadians now seek to defend the integrity of Canada against the United States by defining their own country as more humane, more equalitarian, more democratic, and more anti-imperialist than the United States. Many Canadians now view their country as more "leftist" or liberal in its institutions and international objectives than the United States. Whether this shift in the definition of the character of Canada's chief reference group, the United States, will also affect Canadian values, remains to be seen. Ironically, the shift in Canada's self-image from that of a nation to the right of the United States to one on its left, may in the long run contribute strongly to eliminating the relatively small differences between the values of the two countries. For a democratic leftist ideology is synonymous with the social content of Americanism. As Frank Underhill has pointed out to his fellow Canadians: "If we are eventually to satisfy ourselves that we have at last achieved a Canadian identity, it will be only when we are satisfied that we have arrived at a better American way of life than the Americans have."[96]

REFERENCES

This paper has been written with the support of the program on Comparative National Development of the Institutes of International Studies and Industrial Relations of the University of California at Berkeley. I am indebted to Sandra Betsch for research assistance.

1 Because of the absence of clear indicators and the overlap with the equalitarian–elitist dimensions, the specificity–diffuseness pattern variable is not discussed in this paper which compares only Canada and the United States. For reasons of parsimony, I ignore Parsons' other pattern variables—affectivity–affective neutrality and instrumental–consummatory distinctions. See Talcott Parsons, *The Social System* (Glencoe: The Free Press, 1951), pp. 58-67. See also Parsons' recent elaboration of the pattern variables in "Pattern Variables Revisited," *American Sociological Review*, 25 (1960), 467-83.

2 S. M. Lipset, "The Value Patterns of Democracy: A Case Study in

Comparative Analysis," *American Sociological Review*, 28 (1963), 515-31. See also my comparison of the four English-speaking democracies in *The First New Nation* (New York: Basic Books, 1963), esp. pp. 248-73.

3 Kaspar D. Naegele, "Canadian Society: Some Reflections," in Bernard Blishen and others, eds., *Canadian Society* (Toronto: Macmillan, 1961), p. 27. Since finishing this article, I have read a journalistic account of Canada written by an English novelist which makes and illustrates many of the same points about Canadian institutions as I have tried to suggest here. See V. S. Pritchett, "Across the Vast Land," *Holiday*, 35 (April 1964), 52-68, 184-89.

4 UNESCO, *Basic Facts and Figures*, 1962 (Paris, 1963), p. 54; United Nations, *Demographic Yearbook*, 1960 (New York), pp. 182, 191-92; United Nations, *Compendium of Social Statistics*, Statistical Papers, Series K, No. 2 (New York, 1963), pp. 324-25, 329.

5 Dennis Wrong, *American and Canadian Viewpoints* (Washington: American Council on Education, 1955), p. 20; Wilson Woodside, *The University Question* (Toronto: Ryerson Press, 1958), pp. 21-22.

6 Woodside, *loc. cit.*

7 James Bryant Conant is one of the best known advocates of the thesis that technical high schools are necessary in the United States; see Conant's *Slum and Suburbs* (New York: McGraw-Hill, 1961); also, "A Hard Look at Our High Schools," in C. Winfield Scott and others, eds., *The Great Debate* (Englewood Cliffs, N.J.: Prentice-Hall, 1959), pp. 165-71.

8 Woodside, *op. cit.*, p. 19.

9 S. D. Clark, "The Canadian Community," in G. Brown, ed., *Canada* (Berkeley: University of California Press, 1950), pp. 386-87. Clark adds: "Canada shared with the United States in the great democratic movement, with its almost fanatical emphasis upon the principle that all men are equal. The frontier provided favorable ground on which to build an elaborate structure of social classes, which broke down under the influence of the common experience of frontier life. . . . Yet in spite of the strength of such forces, the aristocratic principle has persisted as an important organizing principle in Canadian society."

10 Lawrence W. Downey, *The Task of Public Education* (Chicago: The Midwest Administration Center, 1960), p. 42.

11 *Ibid.*, p. 44.

12 Lipset, *The First New Nation*, pp. 114-17.

13 Paul Nash, "Quality and Equality in Canadian Education," *Comparative Education Review*, 5 (1961), 118-29.

14 Hilda Neatby, *So Little for the Mind* (Toronto: Clarke, Irwin, 1953), pp. 36, 46-47. See also Hilda Neatby, *A Temperate Dispute* (Toronto: Clarke, Irwin, 1954).

15 W. H. Swift, *Trends in Canadian Education* (Toronto: Gage, 1958), p. 62.

16 Naegele, *op. cit.*, p. 27.

[17] One of the more subtle signs of certain status distinctions was noted by A. R. M. Lower, *Canadians in the Making* (Toronto: Longman's Green and Co., 1958), p. 446, n. 11, who observed that, to his astonishment, in one midwestern university in the U.S. known to him, students and faculty actually share the same lavatory. Dennis Wrong points out that "with respect to the position of women, greater conservatism exists in Canada than in the United States . . . relatively fewer women have achieved prominence as public figures." Wrong, *op. cit.*, p. 11.

[18] W. L. Morton, *The Canadian Identity* (Madison: University of Wisconsin Press, 1961), pp. 105-106.

[19] Norman Ward, *The Canadian House of Commons: Representation* (Toronto: University of Toronto Press, 1950), pp. 216-25.

[20] Robert Lane, *Political Life* (Glencoe: The Free Press, 1959), p. 11.

[21] Wrong, *op. cit.*, pp. 36-37.

[22] Lipset, *The First New Nation*, pp. 264-65. Dennis Wrong notes that "one finds less of the frequent American distrust of lawyers as 'shysters' or as ambitious politicians, in English-speaking Canada and a greater sense of remoteness and majesty of the law." Wrong argues that the contrast between the popular culture-heroes of American and Canadian westward expansion indicate the respect among Canadians for the law and the converse for Americans: ". . . in the United States it is fhe cowboy, a rugged individualist whose relationship to the forces of law and order was at least ambiguous, who has come to symbolize the frontier, while in Canada the 'mountie', a policeman who clearly stands for law and order and traditional institutional authority, is the corresponding symbol of Canadian westward expansion." Wrong, *op. cit.*, p. 38.

[23] Dominion Bureau of Statistics, *Police Administration Statistics*, 1961, p. 19; U.S. Federal Bureau of Investigation, *Uniform Crime Report—1961*, pp. 20, 110, Table 36, and *Uniform Crime Report—1963*, pp. 33-34.

[24] Wrong, *op. cit.*, p. 38.

[25] James Bryce, *Modern Democracies*, I (London: Macmillan, 1921), pp. 501-502.

[26] S. D. Clark, "The Frontier and Democratic Theory," *Tranasctions of the Royal Society of Canada*, 48 (1954), 72; see also Morton, *op. cit.*, pp. 105-106.

[27] As early as 1921 Bryce had noted that "The respect felt for the judiciary contributes to that strict ministration of the civil law which are honourable characteristics of Canada." Bryce, *op. cit.*, p. 486.

[28] Henry H. Bull, "The Career Prosecutor of Canada," *The Journal of Criminal Law, Criminology, and Police Science*, 53 (1962), 89-96.

[29] Edward C. Banfield and James Q. Wilson, *City Politics* (Cambridge: Harvard University Press and M.I.T. Press, 1963), p. 1.

[30] Alexander Brady, "Canada and the Model of Westminster," in William B. Hamilton, ed., *The Transfer of Institutions* (Durham: Duke University Press, 1964), p. 77.

31 Robert K. Merton, *Social Theory and Social Structure* (Glencoe: The Free Press, 1957), p. 169.

32 See Bryce, *op. cit.*, p. 501, for a discussion of the greater propensity of Americans as compared to Canadians to engage in corrupt practices and demagoguery in politics.

33 A restraint exercised over Canadian labor groups and not over American ones is found in the "certification" policy which demands that "a union must claim a 50% membership in the proposed bargaining unit to be eligible to apply for certification, and must be supported by at least half the unit members in a vote if one is taken by the appropriate board. Again there are variations across the country, but the fact remains that a union which is a minority can neither be certified nor can it use its collective power to force recognition. In other words, where no majority can be established the employer is protected by law from collective bargaining, and those employees who do wish to be represented by a union are denied such representation." H. D. Woods, "Labor Law and Unionization in the U.S. and Canada," a paper presented at the meeting of the American Sociological Association, September 3, 1964.

34 Stuart Jamieson, *Industrial Relations in Canada* (Ithaca: Cornell University Press, 1957), p. 7.

35 Alistair Horne, *Canada and the Canadians* (London: Macmillan and Co., 1961), p. 245.

36 See S. D. Clark, "The Importance of Anti-Americanism in Canadian National Feeling," in H. F. Angus, ed., *Canada and Her Great Neighbor* (Toronto: The Ryerson Press, 1938), pp. 392-438. These differences are frequently cited as typical of Canadians today also. See, for example, Horne, *op. cit.*, p. 9, "[P]erhaps the most universally valid quality about Canadian speech is its *quietness*. And this quietness points to a general dislike of noise, to a distrust of ostentation, and to a tendency towards conservatism that is distinctly more British than American. . . ."; G. V. Ferguson, "The English-Canadian Outlook," in Mason Wade, ed., *Canadian Dualism* (Toronto: University of Toronto Press, 1960), p. 5: "A stranger on brief passage might mistake Vancouver for Seattle, Winnipeg for Des Moines, Toronto for Buffalo or Cleveland. It would be only on closer examination that the marked differences would become manifest: the slightly slower tempo of life, the less volatile reaction to events, the more sober, more conservative attitudes of mind, the higher degree of sabbatarianism, the greater gift for compromise and the middle way, the stricter disciplines of a parliamentary as against a congressional democracy, the respect for law and for order, the modesty which flows as much from a long history of colonial dependence as from a realistic sense of the place of a small nation in a big power world."

37 Naegele, *op. cit.*, pp. 29-30, Wrong, *op. cit.*, p. 30.

38 Lower, *op. cit.*, p. 426. For a discussion in support of this same thesis, see Horne, *op. cit.*, p. 9.

39 Bryce, *op. cit.*, p. 471.

40 Wrong, *op. cit.*, p. 29.

41 Horne, *op. cit.*, pp. 248-49. It might be added that hotels are owned by the CNR, and now all provinces except Quebec have Hospitalization Insurance Plans; Canada also has Family Allowances of $6 a month for every child under 10, and $8 for those between 10 and 15. See *ibid.*, p. 250. See also Lloyd D. Musolf, "Canadian Public Enterprise: A Character Study," *American Political Science Review*, 50 (1956), 405-21.

42 Maurice Lamontagne, "The Role of Government," in G. P. Gilmour, ed., *Canada's Tomorrow* (Toronto: Macmillan, 1954), p. 125. See also Bryce's discussion of Canada's resistance to *laissez-faire*, *op. cit.*, p. 471.

43 "In the United States the Briton hastened to become a good American; in Canada he has been encouraged to remain a good Briton. Nor has any vigorous effort been made to assimilate continental European peoples in Canada, except through the public schools; as with the French Canadians, the break of continental Europeans from their cultural past has tended to expose them to European influences." Clark, "The Canadian Community," pp. 386-87.

44 Naegele, *op. cit.*, p. 44.

45 John Porter, *The Vertical Mosaic: An Analysis of Social Class and Power in Canada* (Toronto: University of Toronto Press, 1965), pp. 70-72.

46 Vincent Massey, *Canadians and Their Commonwealth* (Oxford: The Clarendon Press, 1961), pp. 5-6.

47 Naegele, *op. cit.*, p. 49: "In public discussions of New Canadians the emphasis tends to be on the contribution which the diverse cultural heritages they bring with them will make to Canadian life rather than, as is commonly the case in the United States, on their expectation of life in the New World."

48 See J. M. S. Careless, *Canada. A Story of Challenge* (Cambridge: Cambridge University Press, 1963), pp. 111, 112, 113. Even since World War II, as Careless argues, Canada has remained more conservative than the U.S.: "In comparison with the rich and restless republic [the United States], Canada was a cautious and conservative country: cautious because her path was harder, more conservative because of her closer bonds with the Old World, and the stronger power of traditions brought from Britain and France." Careless, *op. cit.*, p. 405.

49 A. R. M. Lower, *From Colony to Nation* (Toronto: Longmans, Green and Co., 1946), p. 114.

50 Careless, *op. cit.*, pp. 111-13.

51 J. Bartlett Brebner, *Canada* (Ann Arbor: University of Michigan Press, 1960), p. 107. See on this point, Careless, *op. cit.*, p. 150: "The English influence also tended to work in this direction. English gentlemen who entered the government service or the dominant Church of England brought a decided belief in class distinctions with them and a dislike of 'levelling' democracy." Frank Underhill, *In Search of Canadian*

Liberalism (Toronto: The Macmillan Company of Canada, 1960), esp. p. 12, notes that "the mental climate of English Canada in its early formative years was determined by men who were fleeing from the practical application of the doctrines that all men are born equal and are endowed by their creator with certain inalienable rights. . . ."

[52] See George M. Wrong, *The United States and Canada* (New York: The Abingdon Press, 1921), pp. 54-55, 57, 63.

[53] Sir Robert Falconer, *The United States as Neighbour* (Cambridge: Cambridge University Press, 1925), p. 23. Or as Brady has put it, "To remain British the colony must remain French." See his "Canada and the Model of Westminster," p. 61.

[54] Harold Innis, *Essays in Canadian Economic History* (Toronto: University of Toronto Press, 1956), p. 385.

[55] Clark, *The Developing Canadian Community* (Toronto: University of Toronto Press, 1962), p. 192. See also, Bruce Dunlop, "The Law of Torts," in Edward McWhinney, ed., *Canadian Jurisprudence* (Toronto: Carswell Co., 1958, p. 145; "In Canada, as in the United States, legal institutions began simply as offshoots of the parent organ in the mother country. In the United States, however, there was a revolution and reaction to everything British. The Americans retained the Common Law but acquired an independence of approach. Canadians, on the other hand, continued to look to England as the fountain-head. In fact, the revolution that set American jurisprudence free may have heightened the tendency of Canadian courts to use the English line. What was being done by the Americans was revolutionary, radical, not to be trusted."

[56] Clark, *The Developing Canadian Community,* p. 194.

[57] W. L. Morton, "The Extension of the Franchise in Canada," *Report of the Canadian Historical Association* (Toronto: University of Toronto Press, 1943), p. 76.

[58] *Ibid.*

[59] "Behind the spreading of national consciousness there was at work perhaps a deeper change—a new *value* assigned to people *as they are,* or as they can become, with as much diversity of interlocking roles as will not destroy or stifle any of their personalities. After 1750 we find new and higher values assigned in certain advanced countries to children and women; to the poor and the sick; to slaves and peasants; to colored races and submerged nationalities. . . ." Karl Deutsch, *Nationalism and Social Communication* (New York: John Wiley, 1953), pp. 153-55. A study of American Tories in the Revolution concludes: "If there were any serious consequences to America from the silencing and expulsion of the Loyalists, they were certainly not social or, in the narrow sense, political consequences. Rather they were philosophical consequences: the Tories' organic conservatism represented a current of thought that failed to reappear in America after the Revolution. A substantial part of the whole spectrum of European social and political philosophy seemed to slip

62

outside the American perspective." William H. Nelson, *The American
Tory* (New York: Oxford University Press, 1961), pp. 189-90.

60 Lane, *op. cit.*, p. 12.

61 Lipset, *The First New Nation*, pp. 82-90.

62 S. D. Clark, *Movements of Political Protest in Canada* (Toronto:
University of Toronto Press, 1959), p. 3; see also Underhill, *op. cit.*, p. 12;
Lower, *From Colony to Nation*, pp. 84-85.

63 Porter, *op. cit.*, p. 370.

64 Timothy L. Smith, *Revivalism and Social Reform in Mid-Nineteenth
Century America* (New York: Abingdon Press, 1957), pp. 24-25.

65 J. Franklin Jameson, *The American Revolution Considered as a
Social Movement* (Princeton, N.J.: Princeton University Press, 1926),
p. 157.

66 Smith, *op. cit.*, pp. 88-89. Smith concludes that the Calvinist belief
in predestination "could hardly survive amidst the evangelists' earnest
entreaties to 'come to Jesus.' "

67 Philip Schaff, *America: A Sketch of the Political, Social, and Religious
Character of the United States of North America* (New York: C. Scribner,
1855), p. 259.

68 Alexis de Tocqueville, *Democracy in America*, II (New York: Vintage
Books, 1954), p. 312.

69 Lipset, *The First New Nation*, pp. 164-66.

70 Clark, "The Canadian Community," p. 388.

71 Dennis Wrong, *op. cit.*, p. 10.

72 Smith, *op. cit.*, pp. 88-89.

73 A. R. M. Lower, "Religion and Religious Institutions," in Brown,
op. cit., p. 465.

74 Clark, *The Developing Canadian Community*, pp. 173-74.

75 *Ibid.*, p. 178.

76 C. E. Silcox, *Church Union in Canada* (New York: Institute of Social
and Religious Research, 1933).

77 Edgar W. McInnis, *The Unguarded Frontier* (Garden City: Double-
day Doran and Company, 1942), p. 307. The lawlessness that overflowed
into Canada was quickly wiped out by the Northwest Mounted Police:
" 'An imaginary line,' wrote a later westerner, 'separated Canada from
the United States for a distance of 800 miles. South of that line strategic
points were garrisoned by thousands of United States soldiers; an almost
continuous condition of Indian warfare prevailed, and the white population in large measure ran free of the restraints of established authority.
There had been an overflow of 'bad men' from Montana into what is
now southern Alberta and southwestern Saskatchewan, who repeated in
Canada the exploits by which they had made Montana infamous. In
large measure the world took it for granted that lawlessness must accompany pioneer conditions. Canada's Mounted Police was the challenge
to that idea.' "

78 *Ibid.*, pp. 307-308.

79 *Loc. cit.*

80 Brebner, *op. cit.*, p. 255; Bryce, *op. cit.*, pp. 486-87. Paul F. Sharp, "Three Frontiers: Some Comparative Studies of Canadian, American and Australian Settlement," *Pacific Historical Review*, 24 (1955), 373-74.

81 A. R. M. Lower, "Education in a Growing Canada," in Joseph Katz, ed., *Canadian Education* (Toronto: McGraw Hill Co. of Canada, 1956), p.8.

82 Clark, "The Frontier and Democratic Theory," p. 66.

83 *Ibid.*, p. 68.

84 John Pengwerne Matthews, *Tradition in Exile* (Toronto: University of Toronto Press, 1962), p. 38; see also Claude T. Bissell, "A Common Ancestry: Literature in Australia and Canada," *University of Toronto Quarterly*, 25 (1956), 133-34.

85 Clark, *The Developing Canadian Community*, p. 103.

86 Lamontagne, *op. cit.*, p. 124.

87 Dennis Wrong, *op. cit.*, p. 29; Horne, *op. cit.*, pp. 239-40; Edgar McInnis, "The People," in Brown, *op. cit.*, pp. 30-31; Lamontagne, *op. cit.*, p. 125.

88 Frank H. Underhill, "The Image of Canada," address given at the University of New Brunswick Founders' Day, March 8, 1962.

89 Clark, "The Importance of Anti-Americanism in Canadian National Feeling," p. 243.

90 On the identification of Canadian writers with British models see Matthews, *op. cit.*, pp. 40, 58-59.

91 Bissell, *op. cit.*, pp. 133-34.

92 Massey, *op. cit.*, p. 19.

93 The concern of Canadians with the large amount of American investment is based not only on the historical insecurity of Canada vis-a-vis its more powerful neighbor. It is interesting to note that Americans owned 44 percent of Canadian manufacturing industry in 1959 and that America has more money invested in Canada than in any other world area. See Norman L. Nicholson, *Canada in the American Community* (Princeton, N.J.: Van Nostrand Company, Inc., 1963), p. 119.

94 Harry G. Johnson, "Problems of Canadian Nationalism," *International Journal*, 16 (Summer 1961), 238-49.

95 S. D. Clark, "Canada and Her Great Neighbour," *Canadian Review of Anthropology and Sociology*, 1 (1964), 193-201.

96 Frank Underhill, *The Image of Confederation* (Toronto: Canadian Broadcasting Corporation, 1964), p. 69.

THE JUDICIAL REVOLUTION AND
AMERICAN DEMOCRACY

BY C. HERMAN PRITCHETT

THE RELATIONSHIP of the United States Supreme Court to American democracy has been an issue since the beginning of the republic. The organization of the powers of government under the Constitution into three great branches encouraged the notion that each performed a separate function, and stimulated generalizations about the distinct character of each. Alexander Hamilton made the first and one of the most noteworthy essays in this direction, in No. 78 of *The Federalist:*

> Whoever attentively considers the different departments of power must perceive, that, in a government in which they are separated from each other, the judiciary, from the nature of its functions, will always be the least dangerous to the political rights of the Constitution; because it will be least in a capacity to annoy or injure them. The Executive not only dispenses the honors, but holds the sword of the community. The legislature not only commands the purse, but prescribes the rules by which the duties and rights of every citizen are to be regulated. The judiciary, on the contrary, has no influence over either the sword or the purse; no direction either of the strength or of the wealth of the society; and can take no active resolution whatever. It may truly be said to have neither FORCE nor WILL, but merely judgment; and must ultimately depend upon the aid of the executive arm even for the efficacy of its judgments.

In the limited role which Hamilton foresaw for the federal courts he was influenced by the mechanical jurisprudence of the eighteenth century. The legal theory of that time located the judge in a closed, theoretically complete system of universal and permanent principles. Within the assumptions of the system, his only functions could be discovery and deduction. The only way the system could be extended was by analogy, and the creative role of the judge was exhausted when this task was performed.

Not the least of John Marshall's great accomplishments as Chief Justice of the United States from 1801 to 1835 was that he was able to achieve a role of "active resolution" for the Supreme Court without disturbing the official theory that the justices had "neither force nor will." He successfully claimed in *Marbury* v. *Madison* (1803) the great power to declare congressional statutes unconstitutional, while making this appear to be nothing more than a simple ministerial act. Repugnance between a statute and the Constitution, he implied, should be readily apparent to anyone. The difference, as Thomas Reed Powell put it, was made to seem "equivalent to an objective contradiction in the order of nature and not a mere difference between two different guessers." And twenty-one years later, in *Osborn* v. *Bank of the United States,* by which time his "active resolution" had done so much to establish the foundations of a strong national government, Marshall was still picturing his Court as the weak court of the Hamiltonian analysis:

Judicial power, as contradistinguished from the power of the laws, has no existence. Courts are the mere instruments of the law, and can will nothing. When they are said to exercise a discretion, it is a mere legal discretion, a discretion to be exercised in discerning the course prescribed by law. . . . Judicial power is never exercised for the purpose of giving effect to the will of the Judge; always for the purpose of giving effect to the will of the Legislature; or, in other words, to the will of the law.

66

Marshall's successor, Chief Justice Roger Taney, though differing widely from Marshall in his political views, was nonetheless a true believer in active judicial resolution who claimed for the Court a position "equal in origin and equal in title to the legislative and executive branches of the government." And the Court has never, at least for long, yielded this position. To be sure, there have been periods of relative judicial quiescence, particularly during wartime, when there is not much for the Court to do except ratify the decisions of the political branches. But in more normal periods the opportunity for judicial participation in public policy formation is always present.

If the Supreme Court has been in a position to "take active resolution" ever since the time of John Marshall, why, it may be asked, have its recent activities aroused so much controversy? If this "judicial revolution" is almost as old as the American Revolution, then surely it should have achieved by now something of the respectability of the Daughters of that revolution. Obviously it has not.

There are, it seems to me, two principal reasons why the judicial activities of the past decade have seemed to have an almost revolutionary impact. First, in this recent period we have had our first substantial experience with an activist Court which is seeking liberal policy goals. Though "liberal" is one of the loosest and most abused words in the dictionary of politics, I am going to assume that its meaning here is sufficiently clear. By "activist," the other key word in the statement, I intend to mean the same thing that Marshall referred to as "active resolution," but the idea of judicial activism needs further explanation.

II

An activist on the bench is a judge who (if I may be forgiven some social science jargon) is more goal-oriented than role-oriented. That is, he has a stronger concern for achieving the right result in the controversies that come before him than in the process by which the court arrives at that result. He feels a personal responsibility for the court's conclusion, an obligation to make use of the power he has as a judge to achieve the right result. He knows what the right result is because he has strong commitments to a value system which tells him what is right.

Now of course every honorable judge wants to achieve a right result, but some will be more sensitive than others to cross-pressures which limit their freedom to judge, and will have other goals that may divert their attention from the immediate result to be achieved. The role-oriented judge accepts as his major obligation the skillful manipulation of judicial techniques. He is primarily concerned with determining what it is proper for him as a judge to do. To the extent that he submerges himself in a judicial mystique and thinks of himself as dominated by a role with prescribed limitations and expectations, to that degree he loses the freedom to pursue his own goals and feels a lesser personal responsibility for the results achieved. He thinks he has to act as he must, not as he wishes he could.

This contrast is, of course, much too simplified. Every sensible judge recognizes that he is bound by the obligations of his role. That is where his power comes from. If he does not act within the accepted limits of judicial behavior, he is likely to be removed from his office. Judges must take actions, such as sentencing persons to long years of imprisonment or even death, which no one but a sadist would perform if their role did not oblige them so to act.

There is nonetheless in the judicial role room for many interpretations. Judges may be loose constructionists or strict constructionists in their attitude toward judicial power. One judge may feel inner compulsions to reach a certain result, whereas another finds that there is a range of possibilities among which he can choose. One judge will speak often of the responsibility of acting rightly in his role as a judge. Another will stress the obligation to achieve a just result in the case before him.

The contrast between goal- and role-orientation is manifest, for example, in comparative judicial willingness to exercise the awesome power of declaring legislative acts unconstitutional. It is an obligation of the judicial role to respect legislative actions, and seldom does an American legislature enact a statute for which there is no conceivable constitutional foundation. A judge for whom consciousness of judicial obligation is of primary importance will go to great lengths to find acceptable rationalizations for dubious legislation. But for an activist whose view of the Constitution is strongly affected by his own policy preferences, legislation which is incompatible with those positions appears clearly unconstitutional and he must declare it so.

By the same token the goal-oriented judge has a greater willingness to overrule the Court's precedents. The doctrine of *stare decisis* has of course always been recognized as peculiarly subject to infringement when constitutional interpretations are involved. For the Supreme Court's declaration of the meaning of a constitutional provision, if questionable, can only be overturned by the difficult process of constitutional amendment. Consequently the Court has generally accepted the obligation to correct its own mistakes.

But again there are differences of degree in judicial attitudes toward this responsibility. The activist, whether liberal or conservative, will be more willing to reverse precedents that conflict with his own strong policy commitments. Thus the conservative Court of 1895 declared the federal income tax unconstitutional in spite of an earlier ruling that a Civil War income tax was valid. On

69

the other side of the fence, the Roosevelt Court in ten years overruled well over thirty precedents which stood in the path of liberal legislation. The less committed justice may be dismayed by such cavalier treatment of the Court's own offspring. As Justice Roberts said in 1945, disregard of the obligations of *stare decisis* might give Supreme Court decisions the status of railroad excursion tickets, "good for this day and train only."

Almost as a matter of necessity, goal orientation requires the development of new constitutional doctrine to achieve desired judicial results. This is not to say that creativity and judicial activism are the same. One can develop new reasons for continuing in an old course of action, or for not acting at all. But activists, who typically want to do something new or stop doing something old, are under a special necessity of producing reasons which will justify their departures from established policies. Justice Holmes (who qualified as an activist in at least this respect) had to create new constitutional doctrine in 1919 if the Court was to have any basis for challenging enforcement of the World War I sedition acts. This necessity produced the "clear and present danger test" to determine whether speech could be punished because of its connection with unlawful acts. On the basis of this test Holmes made an effort—largely futile, it turned out—to insure that men would not be sent to jail for speech offenses unless the courts satisfied themselves that the words used were used "in such circumstances and are of such a nature as to create a clear and present danger that they will bring about the substantive evils that Congress has a right to prevent."

Again in the 1930's and 1940's, the Roosevelt Court had to reconcile its intervention to protect civil liberties with its non-intervention in the field of economic legislation, and it created the doctrine of the "preferred position" of First Amendment freedoms. As Justice Cardozo put it, freedom of speech and thought "is the matrix, the indispensable condition, of nearly every other form of freedom. . . . Neither liberty nor justice would exist if they were sacrificed," and so they are on "a different plane of social and moral values" than other constitutional guarantees.

Finally, we may note that when it is necessary to achieve appropriate results, the goal-oriented Court is more willing to get involved in controversy. An activist judge will take the chance of going beyond the established consensus in pursuit of a policy goal in which he believes. He is not so likely to be deterred from entering "political thickets." He is more likely to have confidence that his judgments, even though controversial, are right and will ultimately be accepted, and so is willing to run the risk of some temporary dangers to the judicial institution on behalf of long-range goals. We think of the audacious, and ultimately successful, effort of Justices Field and Bradley to bring property rights under the protection of the Fourteenth Amendment. We think of Justice Black who, dissenting in *Dennis* v. *United States* (1951), admitted that his majority colleagues were nearer to the popular consensus in finding the Smith Act a constitutional measure for the punishment of communist teachings. But he expressed the assurance that "in calmer times, when present pressures, passions and fears subside, this or some later Court will restore the First Amendment liberties to the high preferred place where they belong in a free society."

III

An activist Court, then, is likely to be a controversial Court. And a Court which is both activist and liberal will be doubly controversial. We have had plenty of experience with judicial activism, but it has almost always been

71

of the conservative variety. Particularly was this the case from the Civil War to the New Deal, during which time some 67 congressional and 526 state statutes were declared unconstitutional. Since the Court's goal orientation was toward results that were highly satisfactory to the corporations, the publishers, the organized bar, and the other pillars of the national community, the Court was generally praised for its activism in support of principles clearly embodied in the Constitution. Only an occasional political scientist asserted that the Court was acting as an independent policy-forming branch of the government; only a few politicians such as President Theodore Roosevelt and some agrarian "sons of the wild jackass" proposed to curb the Court; and the warning Justice Holmes gave in *Lochner v. New York* (1905) that "this case is decided upon an economic theory which a large part of the country does not entertain" was lost on his colleagues.

It was not until the Court's holocaust of New Deal statutes in 1935 and 1936 that the "country" of which Holmes spoke finally became aware, as Max Lerner put it, that Supreme Court decisions are not babies brought by constitutional storks. At long last it became apparent that it was not the Constitution which said there was no power in the national government to deal with a nationwide depression, and no power in the states to enact minimum wage laws for women. It was a quartet of conservative activists on the Court—Justices McReynolds, Sutherland, VanDevanter, and Butler—who needed to pick up only one more vote to put their laissez-faire economic gloss on the law of the Constitution.

This period of conservative dominance was terminated in 1937, as President Roosevelt began to appoint economic liberals to the Court. The new forces represented on the Roosevelt Court made it one of the most fascinating courts in American history. The New Deal drive had largely spent its force in Congress by 1938, which was just when the Court began to feel the liberalizing impact of its new members, and for the first time in our experience the Court was more liberal than Congress or the country.

The Roosevelt Court quickly legitimized state and federal use of regulatory powers, particularly the commerce power, which only a few years earlier had been a battleground between the Court and Congress. But soon new areas of tension began to build up around civil liberties problems. There were censorship cases, compulsory flag salutes in the public schools, attempts to limit press freedom, abusive use of congressional investigatory power, prosecutions of communists under the Smith Act, and alleged failures to observe due process in criminal prosecutions. The unanimity which the Roosevelt Court had achieved in approving economic legislation was soon shattered by the challenge of these civil liberties problems. The beginning of what came to be a classic confrontation on the Court occurred as Justices Black and Frankfurter, representing the contrasting positions of judicial activism and judicial restraint, disagreed over the extent to which Justice Holmes' "clear and present danger" test provided a justification for judicial intervention on behalf of libertarian values.

In the quarter century which has elapsed since this dialogue began, the Supreme Court has functioned as the nation's principal forum for consideration of the operating conditions of a free society. In case after case the Court has debated the meaning of the various protections in the Bill of Rights. While the composition of the Court has changed during the period, and there has been some ebb and flow in judicial attitudes, almost every justice has been truly convinced of the primacy of libertarian goals. Disagreements among members of the Court have been caused not so much by differing degrees of belief in civil liberties

73

as by different concepts of judicial responsibility for the furtherance of these goals. On balance, however, the activist position has been strong enough to project the Court into an unparalleled role of leadership and controversy in the continuing struggle for the achievement of freedom, equality, and justice.

IV

This is the second factor in the judicial revolution. We had come to expect the Supreme Court, in the words of Felix S. Cohen, to act "more like a brake than a motor in the social mechanism."[1] The Court's characteristic posture had been that of a barrier. Its most famous decisions had the effect of telling legislatures what they could not do: 1857—Congress could not pass the Missouri Compromise; 1895—Congress could not adopt a federal income tax; 1905 —New York could not forbid bakers to work more than ten hours a day; 1923—the District of Columbia could not set minimum wages for women; 1927—New York could not fix the resale price of theater tickets by brokers; 1932— Oklahoma could not prevent ice companies from operating without a license; 1935—Congress could not pass the National Industrial Recovery Act; 1936—Congress could not pass the Agricultural Adjustment Act or the Bituminous Coal Conservation Act. The legislature and the executive were the motor. The Supreme Court was the brake. This division of functions had prevailed so long that it seemed the natural order of things.

The judicial revolution has changed that. In its dedication to libertarian goals the Court has in several major fields of public policy become the motor, not the brake. It began in 1954 with the Court's epochal decision to rid the nation of the blight of racial segregation and discrimination. In terms of our previous analysis, *Brown* v. *Board*

74

of Education was clearly an activist, goal-oriented decision. Precedents had to be disregarded or overruled. New doctrine, based on new psychological insights and more sensitive moral standards, had to be established. The most massive controversy had to be anticipated. And to achieve the goal set by the decision, revolutions in long-established patterns of social life would have to be induced or coerced in much of the country. Even those who agreed most strongly with the Court's holding that racial segregation in the public schools was unconstitutional must at the time have been shaken by doubts as to whether the Court could engage in a controversy so charged with emotion and bitterness without running the risk of political defeat and possible permanent impairment of the position of the judicial institution.

Unquestionably the Court moved ahead of the popular consensus on the racial problem in the *Brown* decision. But it did gauge accurately the direction in which opinion would move, and its action of course contributed signally to that movement. This was not like the *Dred Scott* decision, where the Court was behind the consensus and moving in the wrong direction. The *Brown* decision got the United States on the right side of history at a crucial time in world affairs. It raised a standard around which men of good will might rally. It forced the issue of racial segregation on the American conscience. Eventually the executive, through Presidents Kennedy and Johnson, and the Congress began to assume their responsibilities for achieving the broad purposes of racial equality, and the popular consensus caught up with the Court. But the Court had been the motor of the social mechanism.

Second only to the social cataclysm of the race problem is the political revolution which the Supreme Court started in 1962 by its decision on legislative districting in *Baker* v. *Carr*. In the 1946 case of *Colegrove* v. *Green* the Court,

75

practicing Justice Frankfurter's doctrine of judicial restraint, had refused by a vote of 4 to 3 to intervene in a complaint about the gross disparity in population represented in different congressional districts in Illinois. These problems of legislative representation, said Justice Frankfurter, were a "political thicket" into which courts should not wander. But in 1962 the Court reconsidered this restrictionist interpretation of judicial responsibility and directed the lower courts to hear such complaints. Only Justices Frankfurter and Harlan dissented.

Removing *Colegrove* v. *Green*, it turned out, was like dislodging a stone and bringing down an avalanche. In most of the states the populous urban and surburban areas had long been discriminated against in the apportionment of seats in the state legislatures. The unrepresentative legislators elected from these unequal districts had naturally refused to redistrict themselves out of their jobs, and since it had been impossible under the *Colegrove* doctrine to appeal to the courts, there had been no alternative but to endure the inequalities and lack of representation. But *Baker* v. *Carr* opened the doors of the courts; suddenly in most of the states of the union the validity of the legislative districts and the state election system in general became burning public issues. All over the country, state and federal courts began to point out to legislatures their responsibility to equalize their election districts, and to threaten to do the redistricting themselves if the legislatures would not.

It is still too early to know for sure how this venture in judicial leadership will turn out. But it is already evident that the Court hâs secured assent for a major portion of its holding. In *Wesberry* v. *Sanders* (1964), one of the successor opinions to *Baker* v. *Carr*, the Court ruled that congressional districts must be roughly equal in population. This position is so obviously correct that it has been little questioned, and the process of redistricting the states which do not meet this test is well under way. It is likely that Congress will soon implement the Court's holding by statute. A bill providing that congressional districts must be composed of compact and contiguous territory, varying not more than 15 per cent from the average population of the state's congressional districts, was passed by the House in March 1965. Representative William McCulloch (Rep., Ohio) was quoted as saying, when the bill was being considered by the House Judiciary subcommittee in 1964: "With hindsight, we probably would have been well-advised to have taken some action heretofore." But it took Supreme Court leadership to establish that there was a consensus on the need for equal congressional districts. Until the Court started the motor, there was no legislative action and no prospect for legislative action.

Following the *Wesberry* decision, the Court ruled in *Reynolds* v. *Sims* (1964) and fourteen companion cases that representatives in both houses of all the state legislatures must be elected from equal population districts. This was a much more controversial position, for in most states representation in at least one of the houses has traditionally been on the basis of area or governmental units rather than population. In some states equal population districts do not exist for either house. At this point it is not yet certain whether a legislative counterattack on the Court's ruling will succeed. Congress is considering the Dirksen constitutional amendment which would allow states to apportion one house of their legislatures on other than a population basis, provided this arrangement is approved by popular vote in the state. If such an amendment is adopted, it will be regarded as a rebuff to the Supreme Court. But its adoption would still enforce the Court's equal population district standard in 50 of the nation's 99 state legislative chambers, thus confirming the most sweeping reform of state legislative composition in American history.

A third area in which the recent Court has been moving toward important new interpretations of the Bill of Rights concerns standards of due process in criminal prosecutions. The Court has always had the task of ensuring civilized standards of criminal justice in the federal courts, to which it stands in a supervisory relationship. But with respect to the state courts, where the great bulk of criminal law enforcement takes place, the Supreme Court's role has traditionally been much more limited. Most of the specific constitutional guarantees as to trial procedure in the Bill of Rights were originally not even regarded as applicable to the states, which were free to develop their own processes provided they were consistent with a system of "ordered liberty."

This position came under strong attack on the Roosevelt Court. Four of its members believed that when the Fourteenth Amendment was adopted forbidding the states to deprive individuals of life, liberty or property without due process of law, the rules of criminal justice provided by the Bill of Rights for the federal courts were incorporated in the amendment and became applicable thus to the states as well. This view was rejected by the majority of the Court in the leading case of *Adamson* v. *California* (1947). But the dissenting views of the 1940's have now become the majority position of the 1960's, as state law enforcement procedures have been brought by the Court under new and more stringent constitutional controls.

A principal illustration concerns the right to counsel. In 1942 the Court ruled that defendants who could not employ counsel could be tried without the aid of counsel in non-capital cases, unless there were special circumstances which suggested that their rights would not be adequately protected without the assistance of counsel.

78

This was contrary to the practice in the federal courts, where counsel was required in all cases. After two decades of puzzling over how special the "special circumstances" had to be to invalidate a conviction in the absence of counsel, the Court in 1963 unanimously abandoned this effort, in the famous case of *Gideon* v. *Wainwright,* in favor of a holding that counsel must be provided in all state prosecutions where defendants are unable to employ counsel. Many states had already voluntarily adopted this practice, and the Court's decision was generally welcomed in legal circles. It even stimulated action toward improving the previously existing, but often inadequate, system of legal representation for indigents in the federal courts.[2]

In other areas of state criminal justice, judicial efforts to develop stricter constitutional standards of fair trial have been enormously accelerated and broadened by the recent Court, so that today a system of constitutional restraints covers almost every aspect of state criminal law enforcement, from arrest through trial and sentence to appeal. Naturally this has not come about without controversy and resistance. There are many who feel that the Court has dangerously handicapped the process of law enforcement by overly-protective standards, and as with racial segregation and legislative representation, the last word has not yet been said.

No mention has yet been made of the Court's adventures with the religious freedom and establishment clauses of the First Amendment, which as interpreted to forbid Bible reading and prayers in the public schools have aroused some of the most vocal opposition to the Court. However, time is lacking for a consideration of this and other areas of recent judicial initiative. Perhaps enough has been said to demonstrate the transition from the Court as brake on social progress to the Court as originator of social policy, which constitutes the heart of the judicial revolution.

79

V

This transfer of the responsibility for initiating public policies in certain important sectors from the executive and legislature to the Court creates some serious problems for democratic theory. Here we have, in 1965, a group of nine more or less elderly lawyers, appointed for life terms by two presidents who are now in their graves and two more who have been long out of office, exercising a dominant influence on national policy by reason of their authority to interpret the Constitution. How is such a judicial oligarchy compatible with our democratic pretensions?

Of course this is not a new query. The Court has had to be defended on many previous occasions from similar complaints. Its first defense, as we have already noted, came from Hamilton, who said that the judiciary, even though not directly responsible to the people, would constitute no problem because it was the weakest of the three branches and subordinate to the other two. In spite of recent developments, this is still true.

Consider the many respects in which the Court is dependent on its governmental partners. It must, as Hamilton said, depend on "the executive arm . . . for the efficacy of its judgments." President Eisenhower's lack of publicly expressed support for the Court's *Brown* decision had much to do with the halting progress of the campaign against racial segregation during his administration. But executive impact on the Court goes much further than this. By his power of appointment the President can, given a normal rate of turnover on the Court (Taft had six vacancies in four years, Franklin Roosevelt none in his first term), make its membership representative of current political ideas. He can also organize threats of retaliation against the Court, as Roosevelt did with his Court-packing plan.

80

As for the Congress, the senatorial power of confirmation, though seldom employed successfully to defeat a Supreme Court nominee during the twentieth century, can at least be the occasion for flashing warnings of legislative displeasure to the Court by discussion of recent judicial trends. The Court's decisions, if based on statutory interpretation, can be appealed to Congress by a request for new legislation. Judicial interpretations of the Constitution can be reversed only by constitutional amendment, but the difficulty of this process does not prevent the effort from being made in some field or other in every session of Congress.

The Court can be attacked in even more direct fashion. Congress can change the size of the Court or completely abolish its appellate jurisdiction. In fact, Congress can pass any legislation it likes concerning the Court short of reducing the salaries of the sitting justices, taking away its original jurisdiction (which is comparatively unimportant), or abolishing the Court entirely.

Under such conditions, it is surely a mistake to say, as is the common practice, that the Supreme Court has the "last word" on constitutional issues. Its word is the last word only for a time, and so long as the other branches of the government and the political process generally permit its last word to stand. In essence, all that the Court can do with its great power is to enforce a waiting period during which its doctrines are subject to popular consideration. If the judicial reasoning fails to convince the court of public opinion, it will be overridden by Congress or abandoned by the Court itself as new appointees come onto the bench or as the present members bow to the pressure of the times.

So the first step in defense of an activist Court is development of a modern version of *Federalist* No. 78, stressing the political setting in which the Court does it work, and the controls available to its potential political competitors which keep it from moving too far or too fast. These controls guarantee that the Court will be a representative, even though non-elective, institution, and they constitute effective defenses against judicial irresponsibility.

But the case for a strong Court is not merely that it is not as strong as it may seem. The better case is that a strong Court deepens and re-enforces the assurances that our representative institutions will achieve the democratic purposes of the Constitution. There is a difference between majority rule and democracy. A balance must be maintained between majority power and private rights if democratic goals are to be achieved under the terrible pressures of big government and mass society.

The Supreme Court has unique qualifications for determining and enforcing the basic principles of a democratic system. It is not that judges are necessarily wiser or more sensitive than others to these needs. But they are placed in a situation where they are forced to think about them, and they operate in a context which gives them considerable help in that task. Legislators operate under the pressure of constituents, party, legislative leaders, the necessity to produce a program, the need to act on large proposals whose consequences they can only partially foresee or understand. Administrators operate under the pressure of managing huge programs, getting results, meeting emergencies.

A Supreme Court justice lives in a neater universe, in a situation which is more nearly under his own control and more conducive to ordered thought. His agenda consists almost entirely of cases which he and his colleagues have decided they can usefully consider. These cases often raise issues as broad as those which confront administrators and legislators; but no matter how far-reaching the problem, it is presented in the form of a specific controversy involving real individuals. The issue is clarified and its impact usually sharpened by seeing it exemplified in the lives of persons before the Court.

The consequences of a decision one way or another can be clearly visualized, and reasoning can be checked by an assessment of the results it leads to. The pace of the Court, though its "time chart" is strenuous enough, is nevertheless more leisurely than that of a congressman or a department head. There is more time to take thought, and the end-product of the judicial process is thought—a reasoned opinion supporting or denying a position which has been urged on the Court by the litigants. The Court's thought must make sense in the here and now, but it must also be reconcilable with the long lines of doctrine reaching back to the earliest interpretations of the constitutional provisions in question.

But perhaps more important than any other feature of the judicial process for democratic theory is its accessibility to individuals and political minorities. The President, the Senate, the House all have their separate constituencies, but in each case they are mass constituencies. Only large interests and effective pressure groups have the chips to get into the game of politics today. The courts, however, are open to any individual who has a valid case or controversy.

America's largest racial minority, even after it had begun to organize through such groups as the National Association for the Advancement of Colored People, lacked the political power to secure an effective hearing from a series of Presidents and Congresses. It was only in the courts that its constitutional claims to equal protection could be registered. Without either the purse or the sword, the weakest of the three branches of government proved to be the only one with the conscience, the capacity, and the will to challenge the scandal, the immorality, the social and economic waste, and the positive international dangers of racial discrimination.

The channels of the legislative process were similarly closed to those who were protesting inequality in legislative districts. Clearly the beneficiaries of the rotten borough system were not going to abolish the system that sustained them. So again it was the courts, where the weight of a constitutional argument does not depend upon the number of battalions supporting it, that subjected the naked struggle for electoral power to the rule of law.

Most dramatically of all, there is the example of Clarence Earl Gideon, an uneducated ne'er-do-well, who, convicted of a minor crime without the assistance of counsel, stubbornly and unaided in his Florida prison cell achieved access to the Supreme Court and to the pages of history by a petition printed painfully with pencil on lined paper.

A strong Supreme Court, then, is a support, not a threat, to democratic government. Like any wielder of power, a strong Court may abuse its position. If so, there are ways of disciplining it. If the Court makes mistakes—it has done so in the past and can be counted on to do so in the future—there are effective ways of correcting them. The Court's decisions are opinions offering themselves for belief. There is, in the long run, nothing to support them but the strength of their reasoning and their faithfulness to American ideals.

The legislature and the executive must always be the principal motors in the social mechanism. They possess the purse and the sword. They should have used these instruments of power against racial segregation long ago. But their constituencies did not demand that they act. It is our good fortune, and an immensely strengthening factor in our democracy, that under such conditions an appeal may be taken to a third branch of government responsible to the constituency of reason and justice.

REFERENCES

[1] "Transcendental Nonsense and the Functional Approach," 35 *Columbia Law Review* 809 (1935).

[2] On the *Gideon* case, see the fine study by Anthony Lewis, *Gideon's Trumpet* (New York: Random House, 1964).

THE REVOLUTION
IN HIGHER EDUCATION

BY PETER F. DRUCKER

WE ARE ALL CONSCIOUS of the tremendous expansion in the numbers of students in our colleges and universities, conscious above all that the biggest jump in enrollments is just ahead of us. Today half of the young men of America go to school beyond high school—and the years they devote to their own higher education are steadily lengthening. Tomorrow we can expect a college degree to have become as common for both sexes as the high school degree was only two decades ago, at the end of World War II. And increasingly those who do not finish college will at least be expected to stay in school through junior college—that is for two years beyond high school.

But while the quantitative aspects of this educational explosion are well known, little thought has yet been given to its qualitative implications. Yet they may well be greater than the press of numbers. The explosion is both the cause and the effect of a very great change in the structure of our society—its conversion, within the last half-century, into a society of large, powerful organizations.

Within this century, every government—local, state, and federal—has grown out of all proportion. All the federal employees at the time of Theodore Roosevelt could have been housed comfortably in the smallest of the government offices in today's Washington. Our entire military establishment of that time would simply be lost on any one of our present strategic air bases.

And yet government has not grown as fast as some other nongovernmental institutions. In 1900 the social scene in all countries looked very much like the Kansas prairie—it was completely flat, except for one hillock, the government. The hillock wasn't high, but it loomed very large and stood all by itself. Today the social scene is very much like the Himalayas. Here are the lofty ranges of the great corporations; there the rocky cliffs of the great labor unions guarding access to job and craft; there are the great—or at least large—universities, proud of the fact that they have made a big business out of learning and that they have bigger budgets—and budget deficits —than many a fair-sized country. But there are also the many other organized powers—the farm bloc, the various professional and trade groups, to name a few. Even the churches are infinitely more organized and infinitely more powerful politically in today's America than they were in 1900.

The government may be the Mount Everest in that landscape, but it certainly does not tower above the scene as the little hillock of a government did sixty years ago. Indeed, it is often hard to see it amid the mountain masses. Even more important: the political government is in danger of splitting up into separate, particular, sectional power-centers—unmanageable large bureaucracies, ever larger and more complex military forces, all but independent administrative agencies, and so on.

In short, there has been a drastic change in power structure and power dynamics in our society.

This change raises many questions—of constitutional law and political process, of the powers and limitations of these new big organizations, of the ethics of bigness (an old and thorny question with which the Greek dramatists earlier struggled in vain), and of the freedom of the individual in a world of organized super-powers. Above all,

87

however, this development raises questions about education, especially about college and university education.

Obviously the educational explosion is a response to the rise of the modern organization. For it is primarily in these large organizations that the jobs exist for the educated man—the jobs in which knowledge can be made productive in work and can yield a living. Even in prosperous 19th century societies there were only a handful of opportunities for the productive and profitable application of knowledge. Today job and work opportunities for the highly educated are practically limitless in the developed countries; and most of them are in the new organizations, whether government agency or armed service, university (or should I say "multiversity"?), research laboratory or business corporation. Indeed, the person with an education that fifty or sixty years ago was fully adequate for most pursuits, the person with less than a completed high school education, is today rapidly becoming "unemployable."

At the same time, however, the modern organized society squarely rests upon the educational revolution. Without a large and assured supply of very highly educated people, not one of our present-day large-scale organizations could function at all. Ours is, in other words, an educated society in which education—very long and very expensive education—has become the central economic resource and the key investment.

II

What does this mean for the task of the university?

To answer this question I propose to focus on the educational needs today's undergraduate man student will have when, in a few years, he is no longer an undergraduate or student but a man of thirty-five. This is not a purely arbitrary date. At age thirty-five the American male is at the mid-point of his normal life span—barring such major catastrophies as a nuclear war. He has been out of college about as many years as he spent in formal schooling before he got his bachelor's degree. He is at the beginning of his most productive period.

In terms of his working life he is still young. Of the four decades or more which are the full working life of an American male today—from his early twenties to his mid-sixties—only the first has passed. But he is no longer a young man. He is no longer pure promise. He has reached the age of performance. He is normally well-started towards rearing his family. In his own work he has by that time usually found his niche and his career pattern. In fact he normally has also found his range—if *he* does not know how far he is likely to go, his colleagues and his superiors have a pretty good idea (and so, normally, has that sharp-eyed observer, his wife). In other words, by the time the college graduate has reached thirty-five, he himself should be in a position to appraise what education he has received, what it does for him and what he needs. And he should, by that age, have put to work whatever he may have learned in school and college.

Of course every single one of these graduates is an individual, a person. It makes no sense therefore to talk of "averages." Education like all true experiences is an individual, a personal one. And both the needs of the individual and the meaning of his educational experience will and should vary from person to person. Yet we can say some meaningful general things about this American thirty-five year old man with a college education:

1) The great majority of these men will work with and through knowledge rather than with their hands. They will put to work concepts rather than skills, analysis rather than imagination. Their contact with the

89

world and with work will be largely through verbal symbols of one kind or another, whether words or figures. They will use, therefore, only a very small part of the range of experience available to man—and all of it will be experience at one remove from the concrete reality and from the direct concern with, and work on, the concrete, tangible, immediate world of things and sense impressions.

2) The great majority of these men will work as employees in large organizations: a government office or the modern school and university; a business or a labor union; a research lab or one of the armed services. This has a number of highly relevant connotations.

(a) They will of necessity be highly specialized in their own work. For it is the very purpose of the large organization to create the capacity for extraordinary results by bringing together in one joint effort people capable of superior attainment because they specialize on one small area. Yet whether this specialist is productive or not will depend in almost all cases on the capacity of other people to use this output in their work. By himself all the specialist can produce is a useless fragment, which of course is the nature of specialization. It is only in and through the work of others that a productive whole is achieved. Others, therefore, must be able to use whatever it is the individual in the organization turns out. What makes this particularly pertinent is that the product of this individual specialist is unlikely to be a piece of stuff; it is in one form or another conceptual, and theoretical. It is a fragmented piece of information which only by being put together with other similar pieces becomes knowledge.

(b) No matter how successful the individual will be, he will still remain within an organization, that is within a necessarily hierarchial institution in which even the man

90

at the top is not his own boss but the captive of the organization (and the man at the top is perhaps even less independent than the man some place further down who has to worry only about himself and his own work).

(c) At the same time this is a partial organization, and by no means a true society. Above all, the family and the home are outside. For the first time in history a great majority of people live in a sharp cleavage between family and work. The family is neither part of the work team nor related to the work. The home is a place to go to afterwards rather than, as in farm or workshop, part and parcel of the working environment. In fact the work in the modern organization is meaningless and inaccessible to the members of the family. Life in and with the family, therefore, becomes something separate and apart from work and livelihood. Education has not only to take cognizance of this; it has to provide the foundation for that part of life that is outside of work and organization as well as for the job itself.

3) The greatest change, however, is that the man of thirty-five is most unlikely to apply to his job what he learned specifically only a dozen years ago. In all likelihood he has had to re-learn quite a number of things since and had to unlearn quite a few things he learned in school. It once was gospel truth that what one had learned as a young man sufficed for the rest of one's life —whether one worked as a farmer, as a craftsman, or as a professional. The only difference was in the length of the apprenticeship and in the structure of the apprentice training. But once the apprenticeship was over, one had learned enough. In fact historically we have always made a sharp distinction between the world of learning and the world of work. When working began, learning ended.

Today, regardless of one's work, learning has not stopped with the end of schooling. Learning then begins

91

in many ways. And it is not just application of what one has learned that one has to acquire. It is increasingly new things—new concepts, new skills, new tools, new knowledge and so on. Nor is the learning process over by the time a man reaches thirty-five. On the contrary, the more effective and successful he is in his work, the more new and different things will he need to learn, the more often will his job, his work, indeed, in many cases his sphere and scope of action change.

This is perhaps the most novel condition of Man— and perhaps this is also the one truly distinct property of the Educated Society.

III

The implications of these fairly trite observations are startling indeed for the university, involving radical changes in both commitments and approaches to formal higher education.

The Educated Society demands first new *commitments*:

1) A commitment to continuing education both on the part of the university and of its graduates. It must become standard practice for the highly educated to return again and again to school to learn.

2) A commitment is needed to a different and much more demanding responsibility on the part of both educator and educated. Responsibility to and for knowledge was sufficient in the past. In an educated society there is need for responsibility for the application of knowledge. In the past the men of knowledge were a small minority. And power was not in their hands. "The pen is mightier than the sword" might be called the opiate of the intellectual, for there was usually very little truth to the adage. But today knowledge is the central resource, and the basic decisions are increasingly being made on and through knowledge. This puts the university in an

entirely different position. Today it holds central social power and must assume responsibility far beyond the traditional "freedom to know." It must assume the self-discipline without which its power would be unbearable. It must assume responsibility not only for standards of scholarship but for standards of humility. It must assume responsibility for the usefulness of its work. And it must, as said before, assume responsibility for the application of knowledge.

And the same is true of the educated man who is now the power center—and, precisely because his is a position of privilege, the temptation and danger of intellectual arrogance are both doubly great and doubly perilous.

3) There is need for a new commitment to the education of the whole human being. In his work only a very small portion of the individual and of his capacity are being used. That small part that is the reasoning mind or, perhaps an even smaller part, the analytical faculty. But this is no more than a tiny fraction of man. In addition, the educated man has to be prepared for the demands of his personal life, which is increasingly separate from and outside his work.

There is a horrible example in history of what the Educated Society might easily become unless the university commits itself to the education of the whole man. It is the destruction of one of the world's greatest and most creative civilizations, the China of the T'ang and Sung periods, by the imposition of a purely verbal, purely intellectual, purely analytical education on man in society, the Confucian canon. Within a century this commitment to the purely intellectual in man destroyed what had been the world's leader in art as well as in science, in technology as well as in philosophy. We are today in a similar danger—for we, too, tend, under the impact of the triumphs of organization and of the analytical mind,

93

to downgrade everything that is experience, everything that is performance, everything that is direct, immediate and not verbal.

Above all there is need to give direct experience of performance to people who spend most of their formative years in learning. For in school there is no performance; there is only promise.

This means that we must build into the process of formal education direct performing experience in the arts as well as in technology—and not just "art appreciation" or "history of music" or "engineering science." We must never forget that the great evolutionary distinction of man is not his brain; it is his hand. The brain evolved in response to the demands and capacities of that totally unique human gift, the hand. We must not allow ourselves to let that 80 per cent of Man that is not verbal intelligence but capacity to do, capacity to create, capacity to sense, wither away out of sheer intellectual arrogance. Our society could not survive this, nor could the individual.

The Educated Society secondly demands new approaches to the content and aims of formal education.

1) We must learn to build into every subject we teach, and especially into the highly advanced scientific and specialized subjects, the commitment to communicate intelligibly to the layman.

Almost everybody in this society of ours is a specialist of some sort, whether biochemist or cost accountant. Almost everybody therefore speaks his own language and uses his own jargon. But no one in this society, least of all the great majority who work in large organizations, is productive within his own specialty alone. Everyone depends on somebody else (who necessarily is a layman in all areas except his own specialty) to make his output truly effective, to convert his information into knowledge,

94

to turn his efforts into results. Everyone therefore is dependent on being understood by a great many laymen who themselves are specialists in their own area.

There is a great deal of emphasis today on teaching "communication skills." It is not a term I would ever use, for it implies that communication is something separate and distinct from one's work. The important thing to get across, however, is that it is the job of the man of knowledge to make himself understood—or else he does not produce knowledge but at best information. Our present tendency to separate "communications" from the work itself simply makes understanding impossible. It is barbarous. For civilized people, especially civilized people of high knowledge, have always taken responsibility for making their work understood. To do otherwise is treason to one's own discipline and to one's own knowledge; for it renders one's own discipline sterile, takes it out of the universe of knowledge and condemns it, so to speak, to eternal imprisonment. But above all it is a prescription for being ineffectual.

2) The old problem of specialist and generalist requires new thinking and new approaches. Everyone will work increasingly as a specialist. But everyone must work on making his specialty capable of being used by others. Our curriculum will therefore be more specialized in many ways. But it must be able to teach tomorrow's specialist how to relate his own specialty to the universe of knowledge. Otherwise the specialist will never succeed in making himself understood. Otherwise the specialist will not be able to keep on learning. For typically each specialty progresses by acquiring knowledge produced in another specialty and applying it to its own subject. Only rarely is rapid progress in an area fueled from within. The biologist breaks through into a new dimension of understanding by applying what physicists, chem-

95

ists and statisticians have learned. Similarly the economist acquires new knowledge and power by going to school with the mathematician, the psychologist and the anthropologist, and so on. Knowledge is truly one and the specialties, no matter how powerfully established as academic departments, are nothing but temporary scaffolding, obscuring the full structure of knowledge while they help us to get to one part and to go to work thereon. Unless one understands this, one cannot progress in a discipline. Above all, one cannot learn what will be needed tomorrow.

3) Closely connected with this is the growing need to think through when to teach what. With continuing education becoming the norm, especially for the already highly educated man, the idea that any one school is terminal will fade. In fact the one "terminal" school we will still have around is high school. College should more and more be regarded as the *first* four years of a learning process rather than as the last four years. For the college-educated man should be expected to come back again and again—and he himself should expect to come back again and again.

There is therefore no need to try to cramp into these or any other four years everything a person needs to learn in the course of his life. Rather we should look upon what we teach with the question: when is it most easily learned and most usefully learned?

This is particularly important in all the areas where we try to teach what in effect is a practice: medicine, the law, business, or engineering. In these areas a great many of the most important things cannot really be learned except against a background of experience. Our attempts to bring these things to young men without practice experience, may have been justified when we had to assume that this was the terminal schooling of

96

the future physician or lawyer, businessman or engineer. And even though a great deal of ingenuity has been expended on providing a kind of substitute experience (e.g. through the case system especially in the law and business schools and, much more successfully, through the clinical teaching of the medical school) the results are not too impressive. But now we have an alternative. For example, in my own field, the attempt to teach business policy or management can now be taught when the students have enough experience to make these subjects meaningful to them, that is when (a) they have enough experience to reflect on; and (b) when they have found the need to inquire into the foundation of their work and discipline, that is, when their work requires conceptual thinking of a high order.

This, by the way, is the only safeguard we have against extending the years of formal schooling ad infinitum. Precisely because school at its very best can only test promise but cannot really (except in the arts) give the experience of performance, one cannot mature in school. Any school is by necessity a preserver of adolescence. And it is dangerous and damaging to extend adolescence too long. We will have to work hard on making it possible for people to start work and experience as early as possible rather than try to keep them in school longer and longer—especially as we shall expect them to come back five or six years later—and then again five or six years later—to continue their education, if indeed they do not keep on studying while they work, in the evening and after hours.

4) Finally there is a tremendous need to build into the entire teaching and learning process, and especially into college, the ability and motivation to keep on learning. The most important thing any student can acquire in college today is not this or that knowledge or

this or that skill. It is to learn how to learn—and the desire to keep on learning.

This means that we must teach the discipline of learning: the rigor and method of analysis to bring out the need for new and different knowledge, the ability to define the knowledge needed, and the capacity to acquire new knowledge fast. These things can be learned. Every good journalist, for example, has learned them—usually quite unsystematically of course. But they are not being taught today. And they cannot be taught if the emphasis is on learning what is already known rather than on finding out what one does not know and needs to know.

This, also, means that throughout our teaching we must create motivation. We must convey to the student the thrill and excitement of challenging ignorance rather than the complacency of acquiring what is already known. We must teach how one copes with ignorance—if only because there is always so much more of it around than there is of knowledge. We must give that thrill which unfortunately so very few students ever experience, the thrill of finding something, of thinking through something, of truly *learning* something.

IV

The greatest change in higher education, however, will not be within the educational system. It will be in the role and position of education in our total society.

We still speak of the Welfare State. But we have imperceptibly become something different—let me call it the "Knowledge State" for want of a better term. Few of us realize that we in the United States today already spend almost as much on education as we spend on defense. And unless we suffer major war within the next few years, our education budget by 1970 will be well

98

above our defense budget and will run at 10 per cent or more of our national income. Since Sputnik we have all come to realize that our national strength, if not our national survival, depends on our leadership in knowledge and education. This must inevitably make education central in our politics, our national concern, our value decisions, and our national purpose. Education rather than poverty will emerge as central; it is surely significant that the great Civil Rights campaign was triggered by a Supreme Court decision on the schools.

The American university—and especially the state university, which within a few short years will enroll four out of every five Americans in college—therefore faces a period of tremendous importance, of tremendous opportunity for leadership and innovation, but also of tremendous ferment and controversy. The one thing that is certain is that it will be a very different institution by 1990, a quarter century hence, than anybody now imagines—not only larger but different in its content and curriculum, aims and purposes.

The land-grant college was, a century ago, a bold innovation. It was the first deliberate national policy anywhere to use education at the college level to transform a society and economy, indeed the first deliberate attempt anywhere at economic development of a largely pre-industrial, largely dirt-poor society. It was successful beyond the wildest imaginings of its originators.

Now, propelled by our past success, we are embarking on an even bolder venture, the Educated Society, in which the university and the knowledge it generates and conveys will become society's center. And our acceptance of the responsibility, and our seriousness and willingness to learn and to change will become decisive for the strength, the freedom and the quality of our society and of the individual—citizen as well as person—within it.